heraldry

HERALDRY

JULIAN FRANKLYN

DRAWINGS BY ALAN KEITH-HILL

SOUTH BRUNSWICK • NEW YORK-A. S. BARNES AND COMPANY

929. 6
F

A.S. Barnes and Company, Inc.
Cranbury, New Jersey 08512

ISBN:0-498-06683-5
Printed in the United States of America

Contents

To All and Singular

1

2

as well male as female, being by the years of their age 'twixt seven and seventy, little more or less, *this book is presenting Arms.* Not as the sentry with his rifle salutes all senior officers but rather as the favourite Uncle presents alms; that is to say, generously and with joy in the giving.

Heraldry is a vivid Gothic art, the epitome of pure design; it is the insignia of a gentleman, an honour emanating from the Crown which is the fount of all honour. It identifies a man with his ancestors, it proclaims marital alliances and the union of estates: it declares noble service to the Sovereign and sustains pride of race.

The graphic glory of Heraldry flames in the exquisite glass of the great cathedral's lights, printing a patchwork of vivid hues upon the dim grey stone within: the marble warrior, cold upon his ancient tomb, is identified forever by his carven shield.

Heraldry sings its own song in resounding cadences, in words that have wandered out of the Middle Ages into the mechanized now; each term in its turn is a glittering gem, every sentence a poem. The auditory pleasure of Heraldry is as great as the visual.

Armorial Banners, borne aloft in battle and in tournaments when Richard rode to the Holy Land and when Henry conquered at Agincourt, ride the wind today and tell their thrilling tales of heroism, of endurance, of achievement; the insignia of the Ancient Guilds, of the Chartered Cities, of the Barons and the Bishops, are still in use, shining with silver and with gold, gleaming in crimson or emerald, guaranteeing the integrity and purpose of their owners.

The lion and the unicorn, the eagle and the fleur-de-lis; the familiar figures of Heraldry enliven the prosaic work-a-day world of the twentieth century no less than they did that of the twelfth. The Kings of Arms, the Heralds, the Pursuivants, privileged to wear the 'Queen's Coat' – the tabard of the Royal Arms of Her Majesty – still make proclamations. They still organise State processions and still 'devise and grant' to Her Majesty's worthy subjects Shields of Arms for the use of themselves and their heirs and descendants forever by Royal Letters Patent commencing with the arresting words:

'To All and Singular unto whom these Presents do come . . . greeting.'

London   JULIAN FRANKLYN

NOTE

Municipal arms mentioned in this book may have gone into abeyance due to the reorganization of Local Government.

The Illustrations

THE illustrations in this book fall into three groups. First, there are shields depicted in solid black and white. The object of this 'heavy' treatment is to emphasize, particularly for the beginner, the strength and beauty, the eloquence, and austerity of armorial composition.

The second group is the shields printed in colour. When the eye of the novice has become conditioned to armorial display, the vivid, highly contrasting colour-scheme will be more highly appreciated than it would have been had the coloured shields appeared first.

The third group, following the colour-plates, consists of drawings in open line. These have been provided to enable the student to paint them in heraldic colours. Apart from the pride of achievement that may justly be felt by all who complete the painting, it will constitute an exercise in heraldic art. The next step is to draw and paint from blazon.

The water-colours most suited to heraldic painting are yellow ochre for *Or*, aquamarine or cobalt for *azure;* vermilion for *gules;* emerald for *vert. Purpure* is hardly worth buying – it is likely to dry up before it is opened, but if it should by chance be wanted, the colour is purple-lake. Opinions differ on *sable:* one artist declares that waterproof Indian ink is the only satisfactory pigment, another prefers black paint.

For argent, the best thing to use is nothing at all, the paper is white enough. Chinese white may be employed, but metallic paints should be avoided. White is time-honoured for argent.

We wish our readers success – pleasure we know will be theirs; from this beginning may evolve a competent Herald Painter.

Before leaving the subject I wish to record my very deep gratitude to Alan Keith-Hill, who, in spite of severe illness, and in addition to a very heavy programme of other work, did courageously undertake to make the drawings for this book.

heraldry

Origin and Development

3

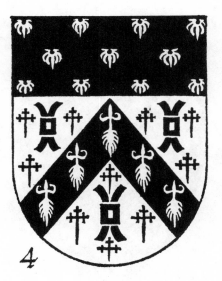

4

THE not very second-hand book published at seven shillings and sixpence and now offered for one penny bore the attractive title, *How to do your own Ancestors*. It began by pointing out that everyone's pedigree goes back to Adam, which is, of course, true: unless it happens that Darwin was correct.

The boy who flicked over the pages felt a mounting ambition: not, one should hasten to explain, to trace his ancestors to Adam; it would be far enough to reach one of the Companions of the Conqueror. This is a very common ambition, and its fulfilment is not absolutely beyond the bounds of possibility.

The boy thought of various slots into which one can put pennies and continued to turn the pages. His half-attentive eye was caught by the word 'crest', and, having heard his father speak vaguely and proudly of 'the family crest', the boy fell. He parted with his penny and became the possessor of that book which he read most carefully. Alas! It took many years to eliminate the harm the opus wrought, and to convince the boy, now bordering manhood, that he had paid far too much for it; that the penny would have been better in any slot.

Perhaps the greatest wrong the publication did was fail to make clear that a 'badge' (which the boy wore for his school) is not a 'crest', and that the 'family crest', vaguely boasted by his father, is not a coat of arms – which his father thought it was.

The poor misguided youth spent eight years trying to prove that his 'family crest' went back to William I, and he did not discover that a crest, however antique it may be, cannot be traced so far back as a coat of arms may be, and that even a coat of arms cannot have existed until about a hundred years later than 1066. Badges go right back to the Bible.

We will 'quick march' on the correct foot first, and keep in step all the way. When Harold, the last of the Saxon kings, bravely fought against William, Duke of Normandy, the protective clothing worn by both Saxons and Normans consisted of mail – that is a kind of shirt, and a hood made of links of chain. (It is not necessary to call it 'chain-mail'. You might as well call it 'chain-chain' or 'mail-mail', for *mail* means *chain*.) Over the hood was worn a close fitting steel cap with, at best, a nose-guard, but the face of every man engaged in the combat was visible and recognizable, hence, foot-soldiers could, without much fear of error, follow their leader.

It was because of the nakedness of the face that Harold, at Hastings, lost his life, and the Normans, with no one to oppose them, landed and annexed the island. Had the Battle of Hastings been held off for about a hundred years: had it happened in (say)

1166, William the Norman might have been defeated, and (who knows?) we might today be a really civilized and Christian country, writing beautiful Bibles, and sending missionaries to set up monasteries on the Continent, as the Saxons did.

The reason for this supposition is that about a hundred years after the Battle of Hastings, plate-armour had developed, and practically every military leader was wearing a closed helmet. Such a protection would have saved Harold's life.

The difficulty now experienced by the military leader was that with his head inside his pot-helmet he became unrecognizable, and it was likely that his foot-soldiers would, in the confusion of battle, find themselves following the wrong captain. Something had to be done to enable the ordinary soldier to recognize his leader, and this was achieved by every leader having painted upon his shield a simple device in vivid colour, which became his mark of individuality.

'That yellow shield with the upright blue stripe on it is Lord Ecks: riding on his left hand, bearing a red shield with a horizontal white stripe is Lord Wayez, and following – the shield with the green background and the diagonal yellow stripe – is Sir Algernon Zaed. Thus shall you know them.'

It appears at once from the foregoing that the shield was the central theme of this system of identification by design, and so it has remained through the eight hundred years of its existence. A gentleman's coat of arms was, is, and ever will be depicted upon a shield, and anything in addition to the shield (there is, as we shall see, much) is of lesser importance. It is strictly correct to refer to a 'Shield of Arms': the reason why the term 'coat of arms' is commonly used will appear later.

To no person, and to no kingdom, can be ascribed the distinction of having originated the system of declaring identity by the armorial device. It seems to emerge throughout feudally organized Christendom at about the same time. 'Whose is the oldest coat of arms?' is a question that cannot be answered. Perhaps the Christian king of Jerusalem's – perhaps Geoffrey of Anjou's – no one really knows.

The very last thing that persons bearing arms wished to do was duplicate each other's devices, but since there were but few colours, and even fewer ideas of design, this happened when the men occupied territory that was far apart so that they had never heard of each other. When it happened that two (or even three) such met for the first time at the muster of the feudal host before some battle, it led to much confusion, and even more ill-feeling, for not one of the people involved in the coincidence had deliberately copied the device of another man: each felt that the other should be the one to make changes in the design.

Noblemen and knights had, long before the innovation of armorial bearings, employed officers of their household called Heralds and Pursuivants, among whose duties was that of introducing their master on public occasions by reciting his family history and his military accomplishments. Naturally enough, it was to the Heralds that the task of devising and keeping a record of arms fell, and at length – actually in the second year of the reign of King Richard III (1484) – the Royal Heralds and Pursuivants were incorporated in a body called *The College of Arms* which, after numerous adventures, is still in existence. After this date, and by a gradual process, noblemen gave up maintaining Heralds, and put all their armorial questions to the Royal Officers of Arms who assumed control, and so duplicated arms gradually ceased to exist. There were one or two notable exceptions.

The College of Arms consists of a group of thirteen persons: three Kings of Arms, six Heralds of Arms and four Pursuivants of Arms. For armorial jurisdiction, the country is divided into

8

9

10

two parts: north of the River Trent, and southward of that stream. Each province has its own King of Arms. 'Clarenceux', taking his title from the town of Clare, is provincial King of Arms for the southern, and 'Norroy', provincial King of Arms for the northern part of the country. Nowadays he takes in the loyal part of Ireland and has 'Ulster' added to his title. Senior to both 'Clarenceux' and 'Norroy and Ulster' Kings of Arms is 'Garter Principal King of Arms of Englishmen', known for short as 'Garter Principal King of Arms', or shorter still, as 'Garter King of Arms' which becomes finally reduced to 'Garter'.

The Heralds of Arms, who take their titles from Royal Dukedoms, are Windsor, Richmond, Somerset, York, Lancaster and Chester; the Pursuivants who derive theirs from old Royal badges, are Rouge Croix, Rouge Dragon, Blue-mantle and Portcullis.

Such fascinating titles sound like the names of characters in a fairy-tale and when, on public occasions, these Officers of Arms are clad in their traditional costume, their appearance is indeed romantic. Each wears 'the Queen's Coat' or Tabard of Arms: a kind of tunic having, on back and front, a representation of Her Majesty's quartered coat of arms and on each shoulder a half-cape bearing the same insignia. The headgear worn with this picturesque garment is the pointed laced hat, except on the occasions when the Officers of Arms are in attendance at functions of the Order of the Garter, when a somewhat beret-like cap is worn. The Tabard is donned over Court-Levee costume, knee-breeches, stockings and shoes.

This ancient noble body of learned heralds is not a Government Department: the thirteen persons of its constitution are not Civil Servants, and the taxpayer contributes not one penny to their upkeep. They are Officers of the Royal Household and are appointed under the Sovereign's Signet and Sign Manual. The titular head of the College of Arms is, by virtue of his high hereditary Office of Earl Marshal of England, His Grace the Duke of Norfolk, Premier Duke and Earl.

Time was when England had both an Earl Marshal and a Constable, and Scotland in its own right as a separate kingdom, had likewise. Ultimately, England lost her Constable, and Scotland her Earl Marshal. The Duke of Norfolk's power does not extend into the Northern Kingdom, hence, the English Officers of Arms have no control of the Armorial Bearings of Scotsmen.

North of the Border the control of armorial display is on a far stronger footing than it is in England. The Officers of the Crown who officiate are, in addition to their being Officers of the Royal Household, Officers of the Realm. The Lord Lyon King of Arms has absolute power, is a judge, and presides over his own Court. He is assisted by Rothesay, Albany and Marchmont Heralds; and Unicorn, Kintyre, and Carrick Pursuivants. There are also a number of other titles that may be used from time to time for Scottish Officers of Arms.

All Christian lands had, at one time, a Court of Chivalry. England's went into abeyance in the eighteenth century and much to the astonishment of many people emerged again in all its majesty and power in 1954; but Scotland's Court remained in being, and has its Procurator Fiscal who issues a summons against any person usurping a coat of arms, or committing any other armorial offence. The accused is tried by the Lyon Court (or Head Court) and if found guilty, he may be fined or even incarcerated.

The basic difference in modern times between the use of coats of arms in the two kingdoms (for both are still individual kingdoms), is that in England all offspring of an Armiger (that is, a person having the right to bear arms) are entitled to bear, use and display the arms of their father. In short, a coat of arms is family property. In Scotland, however, the offspring of an Armiger is born with the right of applying for a re-matriculation (that is, a listing) of the father's arms with such congruent differences as the Lord Lyon thinks proper, hence, in Scotland, every man who bears arms has an individual and distinct coat, though it will bear close relationship throughout a family and indeed, throughout the wider organization of the Clan.

In England one can, with impunity, use bogus arms and many people, many organizations, and many schools do so: in Scotland, no one can practise this minor type of deception. In England the Record Books of the College of Arms, which are, in good periods, examples of magnificent handwriting and fine heraldic painting, are private property, that of the College: in Scotland, the Lyon Register is a public register, and it is claimed for it that it is the most accurate, most complete, and most beautiful heraldic record in the world.

In England it was, at a time within living memory, considered 'snobbish' to display arms – in Scotland, at the same period, it was considered abject not to: 'North of the Forth, every gillie is a gentleman.' The fact is – be it England or Scotland – the possession of arms is no more snobbish than is the possession of a surname. There is, in fact, a parallel. The feudal barons who first assumed arms were the first to assume surnames, and both name and arms were related to their territory; later, lesser men made use of arms and surnames and slowly but surely the custom descended the social scale. In the fifteenth century many inhabitants of London possessed no surname, as late as the seventeenth century few inhabitants of Wales did.

To whom, then, in this atomic age, may arms be granted? To every man (and woman) who is an honest, God-fearing, loyal subject of Her Majesty the Queen. No one can buy a coat of arms as anyone can buy a sack of potatoes: that is, by simply placing his money on the counter and carrying the goods away. Be he never so rich, the man who has by morally (if not legally) questionable means obtained such wealth cannot use it to buy himself honour, for all honour – and the bearing of arms is a minor honour – emanates from the Crown. On the other hand, a poor man of integrity will, on petitioning for arms, receive a grant.

There are fees to pay, but such fees are not the purchase price of honour, they are for the remuneration of the craftsmen who, working as a team, have produced the Patent of Arms.

A Grant of Arms is by Letters Patent under the hands and seals of the Kings of Arms: it is magnificently painted, and written by hand on vellum, and is itself a work of art. The wording in which it is couched differs slightly in the two kingdoms, but is in essence the same. It calls upon 'All and Singular' to observe that the person, or the body corporate, to whom the grant is made, is the sole lawful user of the device, and that by the grant the person or organization is, in Scotland particularly, elevated in honour.

The Herald's garment – the tabard – to which we refer above as 'The Queen's Coat', is the clue to the general term, 'a coat of arms,' although as previously stated, the device is invariably depicted on a shield (with certain exceptions). The tabard was a later development of the surcoat – the garment that a warrior in his armour wore over the steel, and on which the ladies of his household embroidered (or depicted by some other method) the armorial device of his House. This, too, appeared on his horse trapper, and again on his banner, hence the gorgeous display at the tournaments, and at other military assemblies in the thirteenth and fourteenth centuries.

11

12

13

14

15

16

It may have been at tournaments that crests were developed. These occasions were not bloodthirsty single combats wherein two contestants attempted to kill each other; they were sports days when the riders in the lists showed their skill at arms. Sports days are gay, exciting occasions, and young men may have rather dressed themselves up – fixed a bunch of dyed feathers to the top of the helmet or, more amusing still, had made a model of the animal in their Arms, and set that to ride above the helmet. Having developed in the tournament it would be found useful in battle, for towering high it could be seen more easily than could the painted shield and embellished surcoat. The very word *crest* meaning *summit* should prevent its misuse: no one whose mother-tongue is English ought to call a coat of arms a 'family crest', but it is an error that gets itself printed in newspapers, and despite the normal care and accuracy of our admirable press, it is likely to go on being printed, for a popular fallacy lives by its popularity, and the editor's duty is to know what the public wants, not to study Heraldry.

The coats of arms and the crest were family property and means of identification – even ladies were recognized by their armorial mantles – whosoever appeared in public displaying the armorial device was a member of the family, not a servant.

The wearing of a badge was quite another matter. A badge is a device adopted by a community to declare its cohesion. In the Old Testament we read of the badges of the Tribes of Israel. The essence of the badge is that the same device is used by everybody in the group. The warriors of the Middle Ages who, under the feudal system, came together in defence (or for attack) bringing into the field their men at arms had, in addition to their personal coats of arms (later, their crests as well), armorial badges that were worn by all their men, and with which they sometimes branded all their stores and equipment. The badge was the warrior's own badge, but it was the right thing for all his men to wear.

In the modern army every member of a regiment wore its badge: now that the regiments are re-grouped, the new units each have a 'flash': this, too, is painted on wagons and other regimental property.

Today every (or almost every) school has its badge that all the pupils deem it a privilege to wear on cap, or on blazer pocket, or on both. The badge is the property of the school: the pupils wear it to signify their loyalty to, and membership of that body. The device may be cut in stone over the outer door, carved in wood above the Hall fireplace – even the book-covers may be stamped with it. In the Middle Ages the badge was the property of the overlord, the men at arms wore it to identify them as their master's men, and the baggage wagons were marked with it.

The man's eldest son who bore the same arms as his father (except for a special mark with which we will deal in its place) might also lead a contingent, but it is possible that his men were distinguished by a badge quite different from that of the father.

A man's daughter could display the family armorial device, but, in the Middle Ages, women were not expected, as they now are, to take part in warfare (the Maid of Orleans was an exception), they had no armour to cover with a surcoat and no shield. The arms of a lady were not therefore correct on a shield and they still are not. The shape employed is the lozenge which, so rumour has it, was a conventionalized representation of the spindle and every lady, whether married or single, was a spinster.

The other shape that was of the olden time officially employed was the oval, or cartouche: this, again, might have either rounded or pointed extremes on its long axis, and the cartouche was generally used for the arms of ecclesiastics, and of ecclesiastical

establishments for, apart from its usefulness, the attractive
beauty of the coat of arms soon spread its application out of an
exclusively military setting.

So far so good. The foregoing brief, and oversimplified historical background puts us in the picture. What we are now about
to do is acquire by easy stages a brief (and also oversimplified)
knowledge of the elements that go to the making of a coat of
arms, and the rules of the ancient art and science whereunder
the Heralds are constrained in their devising of arms.

18

17

19

20

CHAPTER TWO

Geography and Geometry

BEFORE we take the plunge into rules and regulations, it may be helpful to point out that in addition to its being a military necessity, armory was part of the poetry and art of the Gothic age, and its rapid spread and firm foundation is relevant to the mystique of the culture that could call itself Christian rather than National, and that could plan and build the vast, upsurging cathedrals, the sight of which should strike shame into the soulless robots who raise the ungainly towers of concrete and glass with which the landscape is disfigured today. The art of armorial design has retained the glory of the Gothic age, and though we, like mechanics, have to deal with measurements and proportions, we must never lose sight of the grandeur and beauty of pure armorial expression. All the geometrical stringency and straightness must moderate and move to give precedence to art.

The rules that mattered in the beginning were, first, that the device should fill the available space without overcrowding it, and secondly, that it should be a simple, forceful, easily recognizable presentation, the character of which could not be mistaken.

These rules are still paramount: they have, in bad periods, been overlooked from time to time, but their simple force is so great that they recover and bring back the beauty that has been lost.

Today, in spite of the mechanization of the very means of life (perhaps in fact because of it); heraldry is in a flourishing condition, and most modern grants compare favourably in their simplicity, their symbolism, and their exquisite decorativeness with the best periods of the past.

Nevertheless, rules and regulations must now rivet the reader's attention, for the joy of heraldry cannot be fully experienced without a knowledge of heraldry. In addition to the beauty of its design and the brilliance of its colour, there is the exciting music of its merry language, and though dry-as-dust soulless scholars refuse to conform to the pattern of its poetry, the boy or girl (or man or woman) who comes under the malign influence of those people who brand heraldry as 'the hand-maid of history' – or use some other wise-sounding destructive cliché – is to be pitied indeed, for the verbal pleasure of which such mal-instructed students will be deprived is as great as the visual joy revealed in the blaze of glory through a cathedral window that even the most parsimonious of pedants cannot extinguish.

21

22

19

Progress (for that is what it is called), the continuous build-up of scientific development which in our own time has brought us to 'contemporary architecture' (and has thoughtfully provided the atom bomb with which to clear it away), was operative in substituting plate-armour for mail, and the musket for the archer's bow. Britain's first gunpowder-won victory was at Crécy (1346) after which armour and shield, lance and battle-axe became specimens for preservation in the military museum.

When the shield was no longer a piece of military equipment, but merely an outline drawn on paper, there were no practical considerations to influence its shape, and as time went on it became distorted and, in decadent cultural periods, revoltingly ugly. However, it invariably recovered its pleasing contours and today it takes an austere, well-proportioned and very suitable form.

It is about two in width, and three in height; but it does not have either width or height, neither has it a top or a bottom, a left-hand side nor a right-hand side. Its top is the Chief: its bottom the Base. Its left-hand side – as you look at it – is Dexter, its right, Sinister. Were you a warrior thinking of your shield in relation to yourself you would be behind it, and then dexter would correspond to your right hand. Width and height are expressed respectively Fess and Pale, hence, the modern shield's proportions are two in the fess by three in the pale.

In order to describe exactly where an object depicted on the shield is placed, the area has to be divided up into what we will call 'manors'. The entire surface of the shield is the field, and this is conveniently cut into nine parts, thus:*

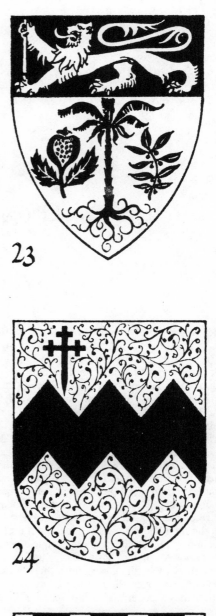

23

24

A	Centre chief
Aa	Dexter chief
Ab	Sinister chief
●	is the actual fess point, but the surrounding area covered by
B	is also termed fess point
Ba	Dexter flank
Bb	Sinister flank
C	Centre base
Ca	Dexter base
Cb	Sinister base
▲	is the Honour point.
■	is the Nombril point.

These 'manors', as we have called them, have no physical boundaries – they are geographical definitions only – but physical barriers may be erected on the field thus parting it. When a vertical line is drawn downward from centre chief, passing over honour point, fess point and nombril point the field is parted, or is party, per pale: had the line been drawn horizontally from flank to flank at fess point level the field would have been party per fess, but the word 'party' is generally omitted, 'per pale' or 'per fess' is enough. Per pale and per fess together giving four boxes is called simply quarterly, or to be precise, quarterly of four.

One may part the field diagonally by a line drawn from the dexter-chief corner through the fess point to the sinister flank: this is described as 'per bend'. A diagonal in the opposite direction gives 'per bend sinister', and the two together, making an X shape, part the field 'per saltire'. If the top of the X is cut away, leaving only an inverted V, the field is 'party per chevron'.

* We deplore the use of 'diagrams', but as this book is intended as a simple introduction to our subject, this one may be justifiable.

25

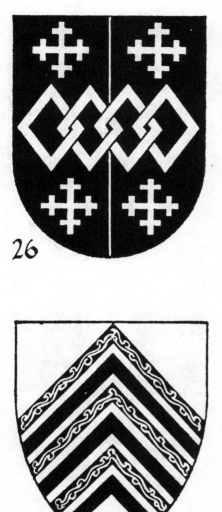

26

27

28

So far the field has been parted into either two, or four sections, but odd numbers are not tabu. A vertical line from the apex of the inverted V to centre chief divides the shield into three parts: an arrangement that may be described in two ways: either 'per chevron, and in chief per pale', or 'tierced [that is, cut into three] in pairle'.

If we had cut off the bottom of the X when we were per saltire and had dropped our horizontal from fess point to centre base, our field would have been 'tierced per graft'.

When a field is parted it generally partakes of two colours, which word, though it may be employed loosely and generally, is not correctly applied to any one particular tint used in heraldry. There is a total of only seven: two metals and five tinctures. The former are the precious metals, gold and silver, respectively named Or and argent. (It is best to use a capital O when writing Or, the metal, *or* it may be confused!) The latter are azure (blue), gules (red), sable (black), purpure (purple), and vert (green). The shades should be vivid, strong, intense: no pale-blue, nor baby-ribbon pretty pink of little Alice's hair-bow. Heraldry is strong meat, its colours manly, and masterful.

It is an inviolable rule (which, like all the other rules has often been violated) that tincture may not rest upon tincture, nor metal upon metal. When, however, metal and tincture are combined in what is called a 'variation of the field' (which will later, and in a more convenient place, be explained in detail), it ceases to have the characteristic of either (or it possesses that of both), and may act as a resting place for objects of either metal or tincture.

This dualism is shared by the heraldic furs which, although represented as repeat patterns of metal and tinctures, are based on the use of biological fur. The animals sacrificed for the finery were of but two species: the Arctic stoat and the 'blue' squirrel. The former, a white creature with a black tip to its tail, provided its skin for robes of office— '. . . to think we buy gowns lined with ermine . . .'. The heraldic fur called ermine is argent powdered with 'ermine spots' sable. The ermine spot has been drawn in various ways throughout the ages, some of the shapes have survived and may be employed on appropriate occasions, but the modern ermine spot is a little slender arrowhead with three dots, arranged in triangle over its point. If the field is sable powdered with ermine spots argent, the fur is 'ermines': Or, with sable spots, is called 'erminois', and sable with Or spots, 'pean.'

The heraldic fur called vair represents the squirrel, and is of a conventionalized form. The shapes employed in its construction are like the contours of a church-bell with sharp angles in place of curves. Taken individually, as they sometimes may be, they are actually called 'vair bells'. These bells, touching each other with their bases downward cross the field in rows, and the spaces between become inverted bells. The metal and tincture employed is argent and azure: the first whole bell in dexter chief will be of the metal, and they recur alternately. In the chiefmost row the bells of metal have their bases downward and in contact, base to base with the inverted bells in the row immediately beneath which are of tincture. If this order is reversed, so that the bells of metal in the chiefmost row are base to base with the bells of metal in the next row, the fur is called counter-vair but both forms (base to base alike, or base to point alike), must be of argent and azure. If the tincture used is not azure, or if in place of argent Or appears with any of the tinctures, for example, argent and gules, or Or and azure, the fur is vairy (or vairé) or counter-vairy, according to base and point contact. It should be pointed out that counter-vairy is rarely seen.

In the Middle Ages the vair bells had curves in place of angles and were about twice as high from base to apex, as the modern vair bell. There are a few coats of arms in which this form appears, and it is described as 'old-vair' or as 'long-vair'.

A development of vair in which the shapes are not bells, but are short, stumpy capital T's is called potent (and counter potent) from the Old English word for a crutch. These changes in colour, in grouping, and in shape of the geometrical elements that go to the making of the heraldic furs are inclined to strike a cold despair into the eager heart of the student meeting them for the first time, but this is a false emotion: the array is, in any case, not formidable – less than half as many as there are letters in the English alphabet – and the reader knows the letters by sight and name without any conscious effort. So it is with the heraldic furs, and with other groups of the elements of design that go to the making of a coat of arms: one recognizes them by sight and name at a subconscious level, and the mental content is acquired with much less effort than is, say, 'the twice-times table'.

The contractor must gather together the bricks, the boards, the sand and cement that will go to the construction of the building; and that, in effect, is what the student of heraldry must do, too. He has to muster the material, the menagerie, the agricultural and botanical specimens that are the elements of the art, but the alchemical magicianship in the skilled combination of these makes the labour of their garnering, and the conformation to the discipline of their geometry a very cheap purchase price for an intrinsic and eternal treasure.

30

29

31

32

33

36

34

37

35

38

CHAPTER THREE

On the Field

EVERYTHING that has a part to play within the boundaries of the field in the exciting drama of armory is a 'charge', and is 'on the field'. To impart substance and solidity it is customary, where appropriate, to add shading towards the sinister base of an object, but discretion is by far the better part of such emphasis – no shading at all is preferable to too much!

The simplest of the charges are the ordinaries: (their full title is honourable ordinaries), they consist of swathes of metal on tincture or of tincture on metal, crossing the field in various directions, and their width is about one-third of the fess measurement of the field. A chief is a strip right across the top of the shield: a fess, also horizontal, crosses from flank to flank over the fess point. Another horizontal ordinary is the bar, which is only one-fifth of the width of the shield and which never appears alone: generally they parade in pairs, one running from flank to flank between the honour point and the fess point, the other between fess point and nombril point, but one bar may appear with a fess, or with a chief, and clearly a bar cannot be sinister, neither can it be dexter: hence we learn, thus early in our studies, that the term 'bar-Sinister' is a crass barbarism, not an heraldic term at all.

A pale is a vertical strip extending from centre chief to centre base, a bend stretches from dexter chief corner down to the base-ward part of the sinister flank, and a bend sinister is the same size and shape but inclined in the opposite direction.

Neither the bend nor the bend sinister is actually bent, but: there is one ordinary that is, namely, the chevron, an inverted V with its apex just above fess point and sloping downward in both directions to the edges of the shield.

A pale and a fess in combination, as well as a bend and a bend sinister, will be dealt with elsewhere; here we must introduce the diminutives of the ordinaries. The chief has one called a fillet which is a quarter of the width of the chief itself. In modern arms it always appears on the chief and occupies the basemost position, but up to the fifteenth century it sometimes occurred alone. The other diminutives are seldom on the ordinary from which they are derived. All diminutives are simply narrower versions of the parent ordinary, and sometimes there are variations in width, each of which is given a specific name, but most of them are useless – being indistinguishable from one another – and in modern

39

40

41

42

43

times they are not employed, hence, we will, in this book, ignore the obsolescent diminutives and omit their names.

The fess, strangely enough, has no offspring, but the bar has: split in half along its length it becomes a barrulet, a pair of which often run parallel with, a little space from, and one on each side of, a bar. Two of these, without the parent bar between them, are always associated; they become one unit, and are described as bars-gemelle.

Half (in width) of a pale is a pallet, half (again in width) of a pallet is an endorse, but the word is seldom used. A pale between a pair of endorses may be described as endorsed, but is far more likely to be described in another way which appears later.

Half the width of the bend is a bendlet, half of that a cost (or a cottise), and this, with the ends cut off, leaving a little less than half its length quite unattached, in the centre of the shield, is a ribbon (or riband). Bend sinister, similarly reduced, gives bendlet sinister, baston (a term not employed since about the fifteenth century) and baton.

Half the width of a chevron is a chevronel, and half of that is a couple-close, this last being an obsolescent term. The second diminutive of the bend sinister, the baston, had its uses in old heraldry, but in modern times this, and the other second diminutives, appear generally in pairs with their parent between them. Any ordinary, so accompanied (including the pale) is described as cottised.

The first diminutives seldom or never accompany the parent, seldom are they borne alone: twos and threes and fours of them are normal; 'argent, three bendlets gules;' 'azure, four palets Or.' A number of diminutives are normally orientated equidistant of the fess point: for example, in three bendlets, one is tucked into dexter chief corner and crosses the fess point, each of the others is about its own width away and, of course, parallel. Their position may, however, be changed by either elevation or depression. If the former – as in the arms of Byron, and of the Corporation of the City of Manchester – they are bendlets enhanced, if the latter, bendlets abaissé. These terms apply to any charge that is either higher or lower than its normal position.

The geometry of ordinaries is of relative importance: if you intend a chevron, be sure you do not draw a chevronel, but we repeat (and will continue to repeat) no heraldic geometry is superior to heraldic art. If the total design demands a slightly wider or a slightly narrower ordinary then expand or condense accordingly.

Heraldic art, being Gothic art, is austere and deeply emotional, but it is not rectilinear which is merely decadent over-compensation for curvilinear exuberance. The lines that part the field, or that create the ordinaries, need not invariably be drawn with the ruler: there are a number of standardized shaped lines, the more important and commonly used of which will be the only ones given here.

Familiar to everybody's eye is the top of a mediaeval castle, crenelated for defence, and what is more, most people know that this is termed embattled. A field per fess embattled should have no more (and no less) than five rising sections: per pale embattled, it will have seven, or perhaps eight. A chief embattled can be treated only on the lower edge (the upper being the edge of the shield), a bend embattled has the crenelations on both sides, so does a chevron – but great care is required to get the apex sightly both above and below. The rising sections on one side of an ordinary are opposite the falling sections on the other side. When the ordinary is required to have the rising sections on the one side opposite those on the other, the term used to describe it is 'bretessé'. A fess embattled has a peculiarity: only the chiefmost edge is involved. If both edges are to be treated it is described as 'embattled-counter-embattled'.

When the vertical lines that make the upstanding parts of an embattled line are set sloping inward so that the rising parts have a wide head and a narrow base, it is dovetailed, and an ordinary dovetailed has the rising parts on each side facing each other.

Had all the rising lines sloped in bend sinister, the line would have been raguly, which, applied to an ordinary, has the rises on one side opposite the spaces on the other. On a pale or on a bend they slope upward.

A line that zigzags its way across the field and has no more than three peaks is called dancetty, and a fess dancetty, having its upper and lower lines parallel, was called, in old heraldry, 'a dance', and the term is still in use.

If the number of zigzags is increased the name 'indented' is given to the line, but the points should not be very small – when they are, it is merely an example of bad drawing.

A line that undulates gently up and down as it crosses the field and which, like dancetty, has three peaks only, is wavy, and an ordinary that is wavy has parallel sides.

All the foregoing shaped lines are very simple, and can turn out wrong only when badly drawn, but the two following need knowledge as well as skill to get them right: we are dealing with one shape that has two names. A line composed of little semicircles placed point to point may be drawn in two ways, either with the arches upward, or with the points upward. This line of semicircles is either engrailed or invected according to the direction of the arches. An ordinary engrailed has the arches on each side facing inward, an ordinary invected has the points facing inward.

This line when parting the field can face neither inward nor outward, hence, in order to standardize, the rule is that it faces in the more honourable direction. This heraldic use of the word 'honourable' means only senior, or the more important, or first, thus chief is more honourable than base, dexter more honourable than sinister (and, in passing, metals are more honourable than tinctures), therefore a field per pale engrailed has the arches facing dexter, per pale invected would have the points to the dexter. Per fess engrailed the arches are upward, per fess invected they are downward. Per bend, or per chevron engrailed the arches are upward.

Two more lines remain: these can best be described by using a quotation from *Shield and Crest**:

'Imagine that a Brobdingnagian coat of arms has been brought to Lilliput by Gulliver, who informs the little men that the line parting the field per fess, which to them is reasonably broad, is a road. As they proceed along it, keeping in English style to the left, it makes a U turn to the near side, and brings them almost half-way back again, whereupon it makes another U turn to the off side and leads on in the original direction. Steady progress is made: the point at which the first turn occurred is passed, when the crazy road makes yet another U turn towards the off side; and when the driver is almost sure he is going back to where he started, it does the same thing, this time to the near side, and he finds himself level with the beginning of the road and advancing slowly but surely along its course.

'These turns back and forth produce equally above and below a mean average, a series of flattened knobs, each the shape of the protruding "key" on a jigsaw puzzle section. The effect is soft,

* *Shield and Crest*, by Julian Franklyn. MacGibbon & Kee Ltd., 2nd edn. 1962.

44

45

46

47

48

49

lacking in sharp definition, in fact cloudy, and that is the reason why it is called nebuly (or nebulée).

'Retaining the simile of the road, nebuly would call for careful driving, but the dangers and difficulties would not be beyond average driving skill. If, however, an enthusiastic geometrically-minded commission on thoroughfares decided to neaten the landscape, and, in order to do so, all the curves were removed from the road nebuly, and right-angle bends constructed in their stead, then the driving problem would be severe. Accidents would be sure to occur and those involved in them would (if they were lucky) go about their business on crutches, or, as Chaucer put it, "he taketh a potent, and on three feete, thus he goeth".'

We have, of course, met the shape potent among the furs.

A coat of arms may consist of a shield crossed by an ordinary, without any accompanying objects. Six hundred years ago such a simple achievement, namely, 'azure, a bend Or', was of high public interest on account of the lawsuit fought for its sole possession.*

In 1961 another such simple achievement was brought to the public notice, namely that of Sir William Worsley, Bt., whose daughter Katherine became Duchess of Kent. It is 'argent a chief gules', but as a rule the ordinary is between, or is otherwise accompanied by, or is itself charged with, one or more of the shapes, or the animals or the plants, or the numerous objects that are to be found in the stock of the Heralds.

Some of the shapes are called sub-ordinaries, others that seem to have an equal claim to the title do not share it, hence, we shall make no endeavour to discriminate, for such nice classification is a matter of academic interest only.

A pile is a wedge shape, one-third of the width of the shield and in its normal position, issuant from centre chief, the apex reaches to nombril point. A pile may, however, be issuant in base, or from either flank, or in bend. A pile issuant from centre chief, one in bend, and another in bend sinister all touching at the point, are described as conjoined. This word is employed to describe other shapes that touch each other.

A little square, about one-third of the width of the shield, and generally to be seen in dexter chief, is the canton. Once again, it must be emphasized that the appearance of the shield as a work of art is more important than the measurements of its component parts: a canton on a chief ought to be a little less than a third, else the chief should be a little more – otherwise it will look like a chief with a different colour on its dexter end. Further, although the correct, the ideal shape for a canton is a square, it may, if necessary, be squeezed a little in its width, or in its height.

If there were two cantons on a chief, one dexter and another sinister, and each was the same depth as the chief, the composition would be deceptive to the eye, for it would appear to be a chief charged with a pale.

An object that may not vary in its proportions is the billet: it is a rectangle being twice as high as it is wide, and which always stands upon its narrow side. It represents a letter, not a log of wood.

A diamond shape, that is not very much higher than it is wide, is a lozenge. Numbers of them may be conjoined to form an ordinary: 'a fess of five lozenges conjoined', or 'five lozenges conjoined in fess'.

A lozenge, out of the centre of which is cut a smaller lozenge showing the field through, is named a 'mascle': one with a round hole in the centre is a 'rustre', but this name is not often employed – it is simply called a 'lozenge pierced round'. When a lozenge is compressed from side to side so as to make it much thinner –

* Scrope *v.* Grosvenor. See *Shield and Crest*, by Julian Franklyn.

perhaps no more than a quarter of the width of a lozenge of the same height, it is a 'fusil'.

A five-pointed star-shape is a 'mullet', but it does not represent a star. If it represents anything at all, and is not merely a meaningless element of design, it represents a spur-rowel (and in Scotland is called a spur-revel). It is often pierced round, and sometimes has six, or more, points.

A crescent in heraldry does not represent the moon: luminaries of the sky have their place but it is not here. The heraldic crescent (unless otherwise stated) always has the points (or horns) in chief, and everyone knows that the moon never falls over on its back, neither does it hang from the heavens with its horns earthwards, as an heraldic crescent inverted does; (there is, however, no knowing what it may do before the rocketeers have finished with it); furthermore, the heraldic crescent is not flat. It rises to a ridge in the centre and is thus triangular in section.

When 'otherwise stated' there are two positions in which the crescent is set. One is with the horns pointing to the dexter, when it is described as increscent, the other is with the horns pointing to the sinister, which is decrescent.

The fleur-de-lis, concerning the origin and meaning of which much learned nonsense has been written, is, in origin, simply a triple curved element of design: it does not represent a lily or an iris: any meaning can be attached to it, but it really has no meaning: anyone who wishes can write a monograph to prove that its *real* meaning is Father Bear, Mother Bear and Baby Bear.

Baden-Powell approved the fleur-de-lis for the badge of the Boy Scouts' Association, and to give it individuality as the Boy Scout's badge it is pierced on each of the outer limbs (which may be called 'petals') with a mullet.

A curved shape that starts in the dexter chief corner, and is about one third of the width of the shield in its broadest part which is opposite the fess point, is called a flaunch or a flanch, but one never stands alone – they go in pairs, one on each flank. To say that flaunches have diminutives might be asking for violent dispute from the pedants, but the fact remains, and must be stated, that there are two other shapes that, without splitting hairs, appear like diminutives of the flaunch. The first is two-thirds of the width (at its broadest point) of the flaunch and is named as flasque, the second is one third, and is named a voider. Flasques and voiders, like flaunches, are always in pairs.

Roundels are circles. They may be thin, as though cut out of paper (when they throw no shadow) or they may be thicker (say cut out of cardboard) but they should never be made to look like balls. They may be called simply roundels of their colour, for example, 'a roundel Or', 'a roundel azure', but each has a name of its own. A roundel Or is a bezant, from the name of the gold coins used by the Crusaders; a roundel argent is a plate, from the name of a silver coin. Both of these are too thin to throw a shadow. A roundel gules is called a torteau: from a Latin word meaning a loaf of bread: a roundel azure is a heurte, easily remembered because a bruise, which is a hurt, is blue. A roundel vert is called a pomme (French for apple), and a roundel sable is not quite so simple: it has three names – ogress, pellet, gunstone. Whichever of these names is used to describe it, the drawing should represent a disc, not a ball. The argument that the pawnbroker's three brass balls represent bezants (which, indeed they do) has no bearing on the matter. The pawnbroker's sign is hanging over the street; the pellet, gunstone or ogress is being drawn on paper. When a cannonball is to be drawn and shaded to look like a ball, it will be called 'proper'. This word in heraldry, used far too often, always means in its natural colours not in heraldic colours: it often also means in its own shape, not conforming to heraldic posture.

53

There is but one other roundel used in British heraldry: on the Continent they have several more, including purple. The final is a roundel divided into six wavy strips running fess-wise and coloured alternately argent and azure. This is named a fountain. It represents a pool of clear water fit for drinking and therefore it is not shaded. Another circular shape that looks like a roundel pierced round is called an 'annulet'. These rings may be of any of the heraldic colours, but they do not have individual names to distinguish them.

Gouts, pear-shaped charges representing drops, and spelt goutte, or gouttae, or gutte, or gutty, have names which may or may not be used: gouttae d'Or, gouttae d'eau (argent), gouttae de sang (gules), gouttae de larmes (azure), gouttae de poix (sable), gouttae d'olive, or d'huile (vert); they may represent drops of water (or rain), drops of blood, drops of olive-oil, or even drops of milk. The object from which they are falling is described as 'distilling' them. When the goutte are de sang, the object from which they drip will probably be described as 'embrued'.

The most common use for gouttae is to assemble them in comparatively large numbers on the field, and although they represent nothing but coloured drops in such a setting, they play a very important role in relation to their background.

54

56

55

CHAPTER FOUR

Variation and Variety

T<small>HE</small> gouttae assume importance when they are used to impart variety to the field, but it is not only they that are so employed, many of the other little shapes perform the same service, and a field so treated is said to be seme of, or powdered with, the little charges, which appear in fess-wise rows. The rule is that there shall be too many to count at a glance, and not so many as to make them either too small to recognize, or too crowded to give the background-colour a chance to assert itself. They may be placed upon the field so that they are all whole, or (and it looks nicer) so that those reaching the edge of the shield are cut in half. It is correct to describe a field as seme of – for example, 'gules seme of billets argent', but it is more correct to give the specific name to such an arrangement when it has one: 'gules billety argent.' Seme of fleurs-de-lis makes 'seme-de-lis': of bezants, 'bezanty'; not, for example, 'gules seme bezanty', but simple 'gules, bezanty'. Plates make 'platty'; annulets, 'annul etty', however, when in doubt, seme of, or powdered with, is safe.

One is not sure that a field seme is to be placed in the category of a variation of the field, notwithstanding that it is actually a variation. The term 'variations of the field' is generally accepted as descriptive of fields that consist of alternate areas of metal and tincture which, when in the direction of the ordinaries, take their names from them. It is not the ordinaries themselves but their diminutives that are employed and, in British heraldry, the number of pieces must be equal. If of six, no number need be stated, but of either more or less (this latter being uncommon over the whole field but quite useful when, for example, the space is reduced by a chief), the number is given. The order* in which the pieces appear is metal (which is more honourable than tincture) first: 'barry of eight, Or and gules' begins in chief with Or, and finishes in base with gules. If it were of odd numbers – say nine – it would begin with Or and end with Or and would not be a variation of the field. It would be Or, four bars gules, and these,

* Metal need not, and sometimes it must not, make first appearance: for example, when there is, on a field barry, a chief of metal, the tincture must come first. A field barry argent and azure, carrying an argent chief would appear to be a field argent charged with three bars azure abaisse, the thin line separating the chief from the first (argent) strip of the variation being invisible from a distance. This illusion is avoided when an azure strip is in the superior position, hence, the variation must be 'azure and argent'.

57

58

59

60

61

being on the field, ought to be shaded slightly in the baseward line. The pieces that go to the making of variations of the field are not on the field, they are part of it, and as the field thus consists equally of metal and tincture, it may carry charges of either.

An even number of palets makes 'paley'; chevronels make 'chevrony'; bendlets make 'bendy'; and, of course, bendlets sinister make 'bendy-sinister'.

A field sectionalized by a line per pale, a line per fess, and a line in each bend and bend sinister is thus separated into eight parts. Beginning in dexter chief with metal, following with tincture and proceeding clockwise gives gyronny – there is no need to say of eight, but gyronny may be of twelve, which must be stated.

In all variations of the field fur and tincture may be used as well as metal and tincture, and the number of possible combinations can be increased by a process called counterchanging. Barry of eight, argent and sable per pale counterchanged means that when the chiefmost strip – argent – reaches the palar line its colour is changed to sable, and second down – sable – at the palar line changes to argent. Barry can be counterchanged per bend and per bend sinister, but per chevron does not work very well.

Paly, however, counterchanges very well per chevron, as well as per fess and per bend.

Bendy will conform to a counterchange per pale or per fess, and of course per bend sinister. Bendy-sinister conforms in the opposite direction.

Variations of the field, like partings of the field, and like the ordinaries and their diminutives do not have to be formed of straight lines. We have already met a roundel barry wavy argent and azure called a fountain. Wavy and nebuly are the usual convolutions.

Barry and paly will enter into alliances with bendy and with bendy sinister to form fresh fields. If the shield is ruled up to make barry of eight, then ruled up to make bendy, the result will be a network of lozenge-shaped meshes. These are coloured, by giving the first whole one in chief the metal, and alternating from dexter to sinister and from chief to base. This pattern of flattened lozenges is called barry-bendy, sloping in the opposite direction it is barry-bendy-sinister. Pallets and bendlets in combination give paly-bendy, and paly-bendy-sinister. When the network is composed of lines in bend crossing lines in bend-sinister, the result is lozengy. A sharper slope makes fusilly, and lines per pale crossing lines per fess give 'chequy' or 'checky'.

That heraldry is not, as some writers depressingly insist, an obsolete art and science, the life of which was lost in Tudor times when the mustering of the feudal host was abandoned in favour of maintaining a standing army, is proved by its incessant growth and development. Not merely do new objects become pressed into the service, but these ancient fundamental compounds, the possibilities of which may appear to have been exhausted centuries ago, prove, in the hands of our mid-twentieth century, learned, brilliant and imaginative Officers of Arms, to be subject to extension. Recently a change was made in chequy. For more than seven hundred years square had appeared under square like the chess (or draughts) board. The 1961 innovation was to push each alternate fess-wise row the distance of half a square across the field making chequy-bonded (as brickwork) or, if pushed from sinister to dexter, chequy-bonded in bend-sinister. Another, less satisfactory, name for it was chequy-masoned.

At this point some writers would leave variations of the field, and perhaps they would be justified in doing so, particularly if the precaution was taken of emphasizing, once again, that variations are not on the field, but are of the field. A field either barry or paly, lozengy or chequy, is quite smooth – no steps up and down; but a fly crossing a field, say, argent, charged with six pallets gules would have to climb up the dexter and down the sinister side of each pallet.

Before we leave the subject of variations there are two items to be dealt with. They may be genuine variations of the field – they may not. In the world of heraldry there are many borderlands and battlegrounds, and scholars who disagree (or are jealous of each other), are seldom so kindly disposed, one to another, as criminals are – we will refrain, therefore, from taking sides.

The two items we have to mention are as follows: when a field is crossed by a number of narrow strips – say eight of them – in bend, having interlaced with them an equal number in bend sinister, the field is described as fretty. Is this a variation of the field? I do not know (neither does anyone else!) because a little shading helps and we are aware that variations are not to be shaded. If the strips in bend are not interlaced with those in bend sinister, but pass over them, the arrangement is called 'trellis'. To increase the effect of wooden trelliswork as used in suburban gardens, a coloured dot is sometimes placed on the spots where the pieces cross. This dot represents a nail-head, and the trellis so finished is termed cloue (anything nailed with only the head showing is cloue): for example, 'Or trellised gules cloue argent'. Trellis, like fretty, is helped by a little judicious shading.

What is emphatically not a variation of the field but, to the uninitiated, appears to be, is a form of artistic embellishment called diapering. It is not even a part of heraldry, but has been used, and is still used, by heraldic artists with magnificent effect. It is a form of repeat pattern added to vivify a large plain area: it is generally in a different shade of the colour on which it lies, and is particularly pleasing in coloured glass. In York Minster there are numerous windows to the memory of various members of the important and historical family of Scrope. Their 'azure a bend Or' is rendered exciting by a darker yellow diapering on the golden bend, and a darker blue on the azure field. Bad diapering (and it is a regrettable fact that there is far more bad heraldic drawing than there is good) is worse than none at all.

Another group of the figures of heraldry that are without a permanent address are the borders. They may be classifiable as ordinaries, they may be sub-ordinaries, and they may be charges. A border or, rather, to give it the correct heraldic title, 'bordure', is a strip, which ought not to exceed one fifth of the width of the shield, running right round it. The bordure is on the field and everything else that the shield contains is within the bordure, except a chief or a canton, either of which covers its own particular area, and the bordure is forced to plunge underground.

A bordure may conform to any of the shaped lines, but a bordure wavy, or engrailed, embattled or nebuly – or anything else – will be shaped on its inner edge only, the outer being constricted by the contour of the shield.

A plain bordure, which may be of either metal, any fur or any tincture, does not have to remain plain. It may, irrespective of the shield it encloses, be per pale, when the dexter half will be of one colour and the sinister of another: per fess, when the portion in chief differs from that in base: quarterly, when dexter chief and sinister base are likely to be the same in colour and sinister chief and dexter base, also matching with each other, but of another colour, it could, however, be of four different colours. A bordure of eight sections is gyronny, and when divided into squares, or as near to squares as the measurements will permit, the bordure is compony (or gobony). In both gyronny and compony the corners in chief are divided diagonally; thus, the first piece of a bordure compony is triangular. The alternation of metal and

65

66

67

tincture begins in dexter chief and proceeds in a clockwise direction, round the shield. Square is the ideal shape for the segments of compony, but if it is found that there will be, say, five and a half squares along the chief it is better to make them more than square – not less than square: that is, make five rectangles slightly wider than they are high in preference to six slightly higher than they are wide.

If the bordure is now split into two tracks right round the shield, the outer track being cut up into squares of alternate metal and tincture and the inner, similar, squares cut into alternate tincture and metal, the name of the design is 'counter-compony'. Three tracks makes a bordure chequy, but the corners in chief are no longer diagonal: the squares run right across the chiefmost strip.

Bordures may also be charged, and in modern heraldry the number of objects appearing will be eight: three along the chief-most section, one on each flank level with honour point, one on each flank level with nombril point and one in base point. Because the number is standardized it need not be given but in old heraldry there was no standard, and any sort of number – odd or even – may appear. When the bordure is charged with the objects of which the field is normally seme, the same terms will be employed – a bordure gules bezanty will be charged with eight whole bezants: a bordure Or billety azure will be charged with eight whole billets.

There are some coats of arms, particularly those of ancient sovereign states and Royal Houses that are so famous as to need no other description, and they give their characteristic to the name of the bordure. 'A bordure of France' will be azure charged with fleurs-de-lis Or, because the shield 'Azure seme-de-lis Or' is known as France Ancient. (France Modern is Azure three fleurs-de-lis Or.) In a bordure of France there should be more than eight fleurs-de-lis – they should follow each other fairly closely because they give effect and do not seem over-crowded, but a 'bordure of Castille' ought to have no more than eight castles: a greater number is not of a pleasing appearance.

Bordures may be charged with ordinaries, but only the ex-tremes appear. A bordure argent charged with a pale vert has the green patch in centre chief and in dexter base: a bordure azure charged with a fess argent has the patches of white in the flanks, level with fess point. This makes one think of a bordure as a shield with the centre cut out, but it is not. An orle, which always parades among the borders, is. Small shields may act as charges on the shield of a coat of arms. Their ideal size is one fifth of the width of the shield and they are described as escutcheons: for example, 'argent three escutcheons gules'. If there is to be one only it will be on the fess point and will have its name changed to an inescutcheon. This, for reasons that will appear later, may also be described as a shield of pretence, and since it must often carry a whole coat of arms there can be no absolute restriction to its size, but if possible it should not exceed a fifth. A comparatively large inescutcheon – one that is, say, three-fifths of the width of the field – which is voided (that is, has the centre cut out) leaves an orle. This may be treated in exactly the same way as a bordure, but it is not likely to be counter-compony, nor chequy, because it is too narrow; it differs also from the bordure in that when it conforms to a shaped line its edges run parallel: it may even go further than that, and conform to two shapes: for example, 'gules an orle engrailed on its inner, and wavy on its outer edges, argent'.

When a number of small charges are orientated round the shield in the position that an orle would occupy, they, somewhat confusingly to the beginner, are termed 'an orle of': 'gules, an

68

71

69

72

70

73

74

orle of sixteen bezants'. The alternative description, 'gules, sixteen bezants in orle' is simpler, clearer, and to be preferred.

The orle, which is about half the width of a bordure, is not the narrowest strip that surrounds the shield. A tressure, which, like the orle, is a little in from the edge of the shield, is much narrower: it is rather less than half of an orle's width. Inside the first tressure, and about its own width away, is a second, and the pair are known as a double tressure. There are few plain tressures (just as there are few single tressures) but so narrow a strip of colour could not carry charges, hence the decoration crosses over both elements of the double tressure appearing inside of, and outside of, but not between, the two shapes.

In Britain's Royal Arms there will be seen in the Scottish quarter a double tressure decorated with fleurs-de-lis. In the dexter chief corner the head is outside and the foot inside; in centre chief the foot is outside and the head inside; in sinister chief the head is out and the foot in; the pair level with honour point have their heads in; those level with nombril point have the heads out, and that in base point has the head in. This reversal is described as flory-counter-fleury – 'a double tressure flory-counter-fleury, gules'.

It will be observed that there are eight. According to some writers there should be sixteen because each tressure is flory-counter-fleury of eight. That may be true, but even so the fleurs-de-lis will occupy the same positions on each, hence the eight belonging to one tressure will come exactly in the same places as the eight belonging to the other tressure. This process of one object covering another in heraldry is described as 'absconding': eight fleurs-de-lis are absconded by the other eight. Another term having the same meaning is 'occulted by'.

A single tressure, when it occurs, is generally decorated on the outer edge, the inner remaining plain, and fleurs-de-lis are not the only forms of decoration: other heraldic shapes may be used: further, ordinaries may be flory-counter-fleury. It will be found that double tressures of any of the colours, and variously decorated, are comparatively frequent in Scottish heraldry.

There is, perhaps, one more matter worthy of mention here. When the Royal Arms are translated on to the Sovereign's household banner – miscalled the Royal Standard – which is of Naval flag dimensions, the double tressure is improved in appearance by being flory-counter-fleury of sixteen, because the narrow oblong space, depressing Scotland's ancient lion, looks empty and unbalanced when its regal border is of eight only.

NOTE: Argent, three escutcheons gules, for the Countess of Errol, Lord High Constable of Scotland, and Chief of Clan Hay.

CHAPTER FIVE

Crosses and Achievements

'GOD for Harry, England and St. George!'* cried the brave young King Henry V, inspiring his men to a renewed onset: and it is certain that throughout the English Host there were to be seen numerous flags displaying the insignae of our country's Patron Saint. Either on shield or banner this device, which consists of a pale united to a fess, reaches from chief to base and from flank to flank.

Famous on land and sea, in furious battle as well as in gentle acts of chivalry, it is enough to blazon this cross simply as 'a cross of St. George', but only when it is gules. When of another tincture – or of a metal – it has other names, the most usual being simply 'a cross', with no description except its colour: 'azure, a cross Or.' Often, however, it is called a plain cross, or a Greek cross.

Because the shield has a greater measurement in pale than it has in fess, one receives the impression that the palar element of the cross is always longer than the traverse, but this is not so; in fact, when a cross appears on a chief, the opposite effect is obtained. See, for example, the beautiful arms of the London County Council – 'barry wavy azure and argent, on a chief of the second [colour, namely, argent] a cross of St. George charged with . . .' (Do not, however, let the ugly shaped shield – seen on L.C.C. vehicles – affect you.)

A plain cross need not extend to the edges of the shield; it may have its four limbs cut short, and each of equal length, when it is sometimes called a cross couped, but is more likely to be given its special name, a cross humetty.

Crosses are often voided. This is effected by cutting a central strip out of the palar element, and also out of the traverse so that what is left looks like a very thick outline of a cross with the field showing through. Sometimes another colour fills the opening and the cross is then not voided of the field, but is voided of the colour, as, for example, 'vert, a cross Or voided gules'.

Sometimes the central strip is cut out from chief to base and from flank to flank, and the cross is described as 'voided throughout'. A cross humetty voided throughout is likely to be described as a cross disjointed. When putting shading in a cross voided, care must be taken: the voids must have the heavier line towards the dexter. Placed on the wrong side, the shadow makes the appearance of one cross upon another.

*Shakespeare, *Henry V*.

75

76

77

78

79

If the limbs of a cross are cut off at the point where they join each other, and the resultant four oblongs are reassembled to form a cross without the central square it is called a cross quarterly pierced: if, however, a small square hole appears in the centre it makes a cross quarter pierced.

Add to the chiefmost limb of the plain cross a short traverse, and it becomes a Patriarchal cross, often quite wrongly called the Cross of Lorraine. This last named certainly has two traverses, the upper shorter than the lower, but these elements cross the pale respectively at honour point and at nombril point.

A cross humetty having the extremes of the limbs cut to a blunt point (instead of their being flat) is a cross urdé: with the limbs split into three and curved like a fleur-de-lis, it is a cross fleury (or flory) but if the limbs are flat, and from behind them there peeps the head of a fleur-de-lis, it is a cross fleurette, or floretty. If the limbs terminate in a disc, it is a cross pomme (or pommelle): if the disc is pierced round it is a cross annuletty: with three discs overlapping to produce a shape like 'clubs' in a pack of playing cards, the cross is either trefly or bottonnée.

Perhaps this is a good place in which to add a remark on the spelling of heraldic words: a final 'ée' or a final 'y' are generally interchangeable, but sometimes the ée terminal suits the word better than y. 'Bottonnée' is a case in point.

A cross with the ends of its limbs split into two, turned outward and pointed is a cross moline. When the two horns are not pointed, but each is flat at its extremity, the cross is called rebated.

A cross having a traverse attached to the end of each limb is a cross potent, but if the traverse is pushed a little way down each limb, towards the centre of the cross, it becomes a cross-crosslet.

A cross having the lower limb considerably longer than the other three which are equal to each other in length may be named a Latin cross, a Passion cross or a cross Calvary. Such a cross, standing upon a plinth composed of (usually three) steps is called a cross degraded because the steps are degrees.* Latin crosses do not reach to the edges of the shield.

Similar in status to the Cross of St. George in England, is the Cross of St. Andrew in Scotland, and the Cross of St. Patrick in Ireland. Both of the latter are saltires: that of St. Andrew is argent upon an azure field: St. Patrick has a saltire gules on an argent field, which was originally the cross of Fitzgerald. St. Patrick was not a martyr, and had no cross to stand as his insignae.

When a saltire is couped the limbs are not cut at right angles to their sides like a cross couped, but the cuts are horizontal, in the fess-wise direction of the field, making what appears like a capital X. In many coats of arms there may, however, be seen a shape that the uninitiated think is a saltire couped at ninety degrees. This is not a saltire at all – it is a cross humetty set saltire-wise. A saltire is not subject to any terminal decoration: what looks like, say, a saltire pommelle is a cross pommelle set saltire-wise. However, this ruling might be condemned as pedantic, because the saltire is so often couped as a cross that the Lyon office will allow it.

Both crosses and saltire may be built up of their diminutives – either two or three strips being employed, and they are generally interlaced in the centre. Such crosses and saltires are blazoned as parted and fretty.

The lines that go to the making of crosses and saltires need not be straight: dovetailed, engrailed, invected and raguly are often seen. This last must be drawn with the teeth on each limb sloping away from the centre.

* Sometimes a cross is described as a cross on (so many) degrees, or on (so many) grices.

Crosses may be made up from lozenges, fusils and mascules conjoined, and the number in each direction will be given: 'thirteen lozenges conjoined in cross, seven being in pale.' Ermine spots, and vair bells may be used in the construction of crosses, four of either being arranged close together but not quite touching with their points towards the centre.

A cross made with its four limbs very narrow at the centre, where they join each other, and very wide at the ends so that the limbs are like triangles, is called either pattée or formée (or paty or formy): if these triangular limbs are narrowed considerably, and instead of having flat ends have a V shaped notch cut in them, it is a Maltese cross, or a cross of eight points.

Had a V not been cut into each limb, but had been inverted and added on, it would have made cross cleché. A cross paty with the ends of the limbs bulging outward in a curve is cross globical: this, with two notches cut into its curved surfaces becomes cross patonce.

All crosses may be varied by having their lower limbs tapered off to a sharp point. When this is done the cross is given its usual name and the word fitchy added. Cross-crosslets, and the various crosses made up of triangular elements, when rendered fitchy are deprived of the lower limb, and the spike is attached to the centre. The effect is to produce a cross most graceful and pleasing to the eye. If the spike is added without removing the lower limb – is, in fact, an extension of, or an attachment to, its extremity – the cross is called 'fitchy at the foot', and the effect is rather coarse and ugly.

A disc placed over the centre of any cross makes it a cross of its kind nowy, and a square so employed makes nowy-quadrate. Neither the disc nor the square should be drawn as over the cross but as part of it – another addition possible to the centre of a cross but one that is not part of it, is an effulgence of rays, like a light shining from behind, and making the cross rayonnant, or radiated.

All crosses may have a very narrow border of their own. This is not an overlay, it must not be shaded to give thickness. Crosses so treated are said to be fimbriated, and since a cross of metal must be fimbriated of a tincture and vice versa, it enables a cross of tincture, fimbriated, to rest on a field of tincture which is sometimes very convenient, a great relief to harassed heralds.

Ever since books on heraldry have been printed, their authors have been conscious of the readers' likelihood of getting very tired of crosses. One,* who wrote his book in the form of a conversation between a herald and a knight, makes the knight's servant interrupt the conversation. We will call our own halt. The crosses here given are a bare minimum that one is sure to see as soon as one becomes coat-of-arms-conscious – there are hundreds more, scores of which will slowly accumulate in the receptive mind, no special effort of memory being needed.

The large number of crosses is, perhaps, due to the influence of the Crusades: but at one time it was customary to attribute far too much to the cultural impact of these expeditions.

The exterior drapery, called mantling, which normally accompanies the shield is said to be of Crusading origin. We now know that it was not, but we still do not know its origin.

Although the shield is in itself the coat of arms, and can stand alone, it is usual to depict it within a setting of additional matter, the whole of which constitutes the achievement.

First, above the shield, and resting upon it, is a helmet. In old heraldry this was decorative and was, to a certain extent only, a mark of high rank. Later – about the Stuart period – various

* Gerard Legh, 1562. *The Accedens of Armory.*

80

81

82

83

84

85

different patterns of helmets, called helmets of rank, were introduced and, in theory, they are still in use.

Shields are described as 'ensigned with a helmet befitting his degree', or else the helmet is named: the Royal helmet is of gold, is set full-face – in heraldic language, affrontée, and has a grille of six bars (or bailes): a duke, or a marquis, has a helmet of the same shape, also set affrontée, but it is of silver garnished (that is, fitted with ornamental facings) of gold. The grille has only five bars. An earl, a viscount or a baron has the same silver helmet garnished gold, but it looks to the dexter and has five bailes visible.

Baronets and knights and gentlemen have a different type of helmet. It is a visored type, with the sloping, beaklike face-guard that may be opened and shut. Baronets and knights have their shield ensigned with an open helmet affrontée, showing its crimson lining. It is said to be of steel, garnished silver. Gentlemen have the same shaped helmet, facing dexter, and closed. From the point of view of appearance, gentlemen come off best. From the Royal helmet to the gentleman's helmet the shapes are very ugly, and when badly drawn, as helmets so frequently are, they look uglier. The helmet is itself ensigned with the crest and when this is an animal advancing to the dexter its appearance is very odd when on a helmet affrontée, and vice versa.

Because of these drawbacks the helmet of rank is, in our own time, being very quietly dropped. Any rank may ensign arms with a tilting helmet: that is the 'frog-face' type, with its horizontal slit through which the rider could see. This may be placed either dexter or affrontée, or at an angle between the two and so, without making reference to rank, can decently conform to an artistic setting.

Resting upon any kind of helmet will normally be a twisted pad (or ring) called a 'wreath of the colours', or a 'torse', or a 'bandeau': the colours being the chief metal and chief tincture used in the arms, but a wreath may be of three colours. The metal always comes first, and the number of twists depicted is six.

Out of this circle of twisted silks the crest itself rises, hence, a crest, when used without its shield, must rest on its wreath, and the blazon must always begin with the words: 'on a wreath of the colours.' (There are, on some occasions, objects other than a wreath out of which crests arise, but these will appear later.)

Descending in a cascade of curling pieces, and draping each side of the helmet and the shield is the mantling, or lambrequin. It twists in its descent, showing now outside, now inside. Before the fifteenth century mantlings were nearly always of gules lined argent (or else ermine), but nowadays the mantling is of the colours, just as the wreath is.

Beneath the shield there is most likely to be an escroll, bearing the family motto, but this is not part of the arms and may be altered at will, except in Scotland, where it is quoted in the patent.

Crests, originally of a nature that could indeed be carried upon the helmet, soon became decadent, and very silly indeed. What is worse, there grew up a tendency to employ the crest in preference to the arms, hence, many people today possess a signet ring of their crest (probably made for the grandfather), and do not even know that it is merely a sort of top-knot for a shield of arms.

Ladies do not display crests, neither do priests. Pope Innocent IV, at the Council of Lyons in A.D.1245 introduced the representation of the ecclesiastical hat as fitting to ensign such arms: small of crown and broad of brim, having descending from it two cords ending in tassels, it is an attractive adornment. A variation in the colour of the hat and the number of its tassels indicates the rank of the churchman – a cardinal's hat is red, and has fifteen tassels on each cord. In the Church of England a clergyman using family arms uses also a crest, but when he becomes a bishop he lays it aside in favour of a mitre.

Among the exterior decorations of the shield may often be seen a pair of creatures – human or animal – who are holding the shield between them. These are the supporters, and are not quite so common as they seem. They may be granted only to Peers of the Realm – including Baronets – or to bodies corporate, as for example, the corporation of a city, town or borough, or a public limited company. Whether the supporters are human beings often in uniform, or the normal dress of a trade (such as miners); or are birds, or other animals either real or imaginary, they need something on which to stand. This footing is normally provided, and is called the compartment. It is a word which, like some others employed in heraldry, has changed a little – obviously, *comportment* would be more descriptive.

In modern times the compartment is generally a green hillock, or some other object on which it is reasonable to stand, but in bad periods of heraldic art, they have sometimes been quite ugly and utterly foolish. It was far better when the heralds did not specify the compartment, and the artist drew the animals standing on the escroll, or on some imaginary twisted ironwork. So long as the supporters did their work of holding the shield, there was little to justify complaint, but the time came when it was fashionable to draw the supporters as though they were sneaking away from behind the shield. They even went so far as to cut them like this in stone. See the Royal Arms over the entrance of the National Portrait Gallery. Far too often the supporters are so badly drawn that even when they are complete, and in the correct attitude, they look as though they are clutching the shield to support themselves, their hind legs being too puny to hold them.

Single supporters, never very common, were more likely to be seen in Scottish than in English grants. The animal usually squats on its haunches and has the shield hanging by its guige (strap) from about its neck. There is one example of a shield suspended upon the mast of a ship.

Before leaving this subject one should point out that there has been in the past a tendency to draw the crest far too big for the shield, and because such disproportionate composition may be seen in St. George's Chapel, Windsor and elsewhere, there are many who declare it 'correct', and expect modern drawing to conform. It is indeed a fact that large helmets, and therefore large crests, were to be seen in practical use during the twelfth and thirteenth centuries, but modern art need not be constricted by the military necessity of antiquity.

In the same category of art, and subject to similar adverse criticism falls the custom of depicting – without discrimination – shields a-couché, that is, tilted over to the dexter. Again it is a fact that a warrior, making a journey, and carrying his shield by the guige actually had it hanging at such an angle – he may, when riding thus at ease, have had parts of his armour unstrapped and flapping loose, and been in numerous other ways improperly dressed. Perhaps, when he dismounted and disarmed, he stood the shield on its head against the wall, but that is no reason why modern art should employ not only poor design, but a style that results in a deceptive appearance which is the antithesis of good heraldry.

In Continental achievements where the couché shield is common, no ill effect is produced because the average European coat of arms is without an ordinary, but here in Britain where the vast majority of achievements include an ordinary, the a-couché style should be employed only with great discretion. It distorts the design badly. A fess looks like a pale: a pale looks like a fess: a cross seems to be a saltire, and a saltire, a cross.

86

87

88

89

90

91

We do not need to copy examples of our ancestor's bad taste, nor do we need to represent as styles their errors in drawing.

The artists of the Gothic period lived in a different world and had a different outlook. Much of their work was unsurpassably good – we cannot exceed it: we can barely equal it, but their eye for design was different from ours, and it is ridiculous to accept even their bad work as good, simply because it is old.

Another affectation of the so-called 'mediaevalist' is to ignore the rules of blazon; that is, description of a coat of arms by the standard and accepted formula, and to talk (and write) in the haphazard heraldic language that led to confusion before the days of discipline.

The reader has, by now, acquired a sufficient number of the ringing, exciting heraldic words to realize that a familiarity with them is worthy of cultivation. The fact is, mastery of the art of blazon makes the Heraldist. A man may visualize hundreds of coats of arms in use in the thirteenth century, and know the family history attached to each achievement, but if he cannot (or will not) express them in proper terms he has nothing, for knowledge that is not generously shared can but poison the mind that imprisons it.

Ablazon, like a chemical formula, means one thing, and one thing only, hence, every heraldic artist can make a correct drawing from it: in that ability lies the difference between the heraldic-artist and the heraldic-draughtsman. The former emblazons (paints) from blazon (verbal description), the latter, at best, makes a neater copy of a rough sketch placed before him, or, at worst (and very commonly), adds a few of his own errors to the errors of his predecessors. Even some of those who can draw and paint from blazon produce nothing that rises to the status of art. To be neat and tidy is not enough.

When coach-panels were emblazoned – say down to the end of the nineteenth century – the painters themselves were often far from skilful, and knew not a word of heraldry – some of them could not even read.

In reciting, or in writing the blazon of arms one proceeds layer by layer. First comes the field which, as we already know, may be expressed in one word: 'argent', or 'gules', or 'ermine'. If it is parted, the more honourable precedes the less: 'per pale, argent and gules;' 'per bend, ermine and sable;' 'per fess Or and azure'. In the first example the argent is dexter; in the second, the ermine is chiefward; in the last, Or is in chief. In variations of the field the metal is placed first: 'barry nebuly argent and sable;' 'paly Or and gules;' 'lozengy ermine and vert'. Sometimes the tincture must take precedence: see the arms of the London County Council where the chief argent must abut on to azure. We already know how to describe a field seme.

Having thus disposed of the field, the next step is to describe everything that is in contact with it in order of importance. Ordinaries come first. 'Azure a bend Or:' 'argent a fess engrailed gules:' 'per pale Or and vert a bend dovetailed counterchanged.' It will be observed that the whole of the ordinary's characteristics are given before its colour is mentioned.

Ordinaries seldom appear in isolation. There is generally something else accompanying them. 'Vert, a fess Or, and in chief an annulet argent:' 'gules a chevron argent between three mullets Or.' When there is no ordinary the premier charge is mentioned first. Which, among several, will be the premier charge? The one that is on (or nearest to) the fess point, and it will be like an ordinary, described as between the other charges. 'Gules, a cross patty argent between three bezants:' 'barry Or and gules, a fountain between three crosses-crosslet sable.'

A field may be charged with a number of objects none of which is predominant. Such charges may all be of one kind, but can also be of two kinds. In the latter case, one type of charge will generally occupy the position of an ordinary, and will be given the status of an ordinary: 'gules, three mullets in pale argent between two billets Or:' 'azure, three billets in fess Or between two fleurs-de-lis argent:' 'sable, three bezants in bend between two plates.'

When the charges are of one kind only, the total number and the order of their arrangement on the shield is stated except when there are three only which normally are disposed two in chief and one in base: 'azure three fleurs-de-lis Or.' There is no need for any further description. Had the charges been placed in some other order, it would then have been necessary to state: 'azure, three fleurs-de-lis Or, one in chief and two in base:' 'ermine, three mullets in fess gules.' When the quantity exceeds three the disposition must be stated: 'sable fifteen bezants, five, four, three, two and one.' The direction in which we proceed is from chief to base. The fifteen bezants could have been arranged in several other ways – for example: 'sable, fifteen bezants in three barwise rows of five each.' Another arrangement is, in chief, two barwise rows of five each, and in base, two, two and one.

The importance of stating the disposition is thus made manifest. However, accidents can happen, and common sense must then come to the rescue. Had our herald blazoned sable, fifteen bezants, and failed to give us their position, we would have to assume the most simple, which would be five, four, three, two and one.

When an achievement is in three layers it is generally because the ordinary carries charges, or because the charges themselves are doing so. If the ordinary is involved a note of warning is sounded by the use of the word 'on'. 'Sable, on a pale argent, three mullets gules:' 'gules, on a fess argent between three crescents Or, an annulet azure:' 'Or, on a bend azure between two mullets vert, three billets argent.'

When charges appear on an ordinary, or when they are orientated in the direction of an ordinary (except a fess), they stand parallel with the sides of the ordinary. The three billets mentioned will have their long sides sloping as the bend slopes. Had they been in bend they would also have been so tilted. Billets on a fess remain upright, that is, palar of the field, but on a chevron an odd number of charges presents a problem unless the rule is known. With an even number, say, four, two will slope in the one direction, and two in the other: increase to five, and the odd charge must go in the chevron's point because three on one side and two on the other would be out of balance. The rule is that the odd charge in the chevron's point stands palar in relation to the field, not fess-wise to it.

When the third layer in the achievement is occasioned by the presence of charges on charges but not on the ordinary, the words applied are, 'each charged with . . .' 'sable, a bend Or between two plates each charged with a mullet vert.' A fourth layer is created when the charges on an ordinary are each charged with . . .

In blazon, a chief has special status. Its existence, and its details, are left till the rest of the achievement has been described: 'Or, three torteaux in bend between two lozenges azure; on a chief vert five mullets argent.' A canton is treated in the same way.

When there is no chief or canton, the border, if there is one, is mentioned last, and even when there is a chief it will be last of the contents of the lower part of the shield. 'Argent, a bend gules

92

93

94

95

96

between two mullets azure, all within a bordure vert:' 'Or, three fleurs-de-lis azure within a bordure compony Or and gules; on a chief vert five lozenges vair.' If the bordure carries charges they must be blazoned with the bordure: 'argent, a fleur-de-lis sable within a bordure gules charged with eight mullets Or.' (If a chief were added, the three mullets along the chief of the bordure would be absconded.)

It is usual to find the ordinary in an achievement in the second layer, that is, in contact with the field, but it does not have to be, and there are numerous exceptions. When charges are in the second layer, and the ordinary is in the third, it is described as 'surmounting' or 'debruising', and the charges are 'surmounted' or 'debruised by . . .': 'Or, a cross fleury azure, debruised by a bend vert:' 'argent a cross gules surmounting an annulet azure.' When two objects are placed in saltire it is generally necessary to state which is contacting the field, and the one in bend dexter is mentioned first: 'two swords in saltire, that in bend surmounting (or debruising) that in bend sinister:' alternatively, 'that in bend surmounted by (or debruised by) that in bend sinister.'

When a number of objects are mentioned and they are all of the same colour, the fact is stated only once: 'sable, a fess cottised between three annulets argent' means that the fess, the cottises and the annulets are all argent.

One of the rules of blazon that does much to give grandeur and dignity to its recitation is the avoidance of the repetition of both the colours and the numbers of objects. This is done by giving the colours used in any particular achievement numerical precedence in the order of their occurrence: 'argent, on a fess gules cottised vert between two fleurs-de-lis of the second three mullets of the first.' The order of the occurrence in the foregoing is first, argent: second, gules; third, vert; hence the fleurs-de-lis were gules, and the mullets argent. A more complex achievement, having more objects and more colours, is described in exactly the same way, and it sometimes helps to say 'of the field' instead of (or as well as) 'of the first'. An object would be voided of the field if it were on the field, but 'of the first' if it were on an ordinary, and was voided the same colour as that of the field;

97

98

for example, argent, an a fess gules, a lozenge or voided of the first. The lozenge has a white centre.

If the blazon is very long and complicated, it may help to repeat a colour rather than a numerical reference to it. Repetition of the sum of objects is avoided by use of the phrase 'as many': 'azure, on a fess between three billets Or, as many mullets of the field.'

When the whole of the shield has been dealt with, the crest is blazoned. It is not absolutely necessary in English (as distinct from Scottish) blazon to mention the helmet or the mantling, but the wreath must precede the crest. 'Upon a wreath of the colours, a fleur-de lis Or:' 'upon a wreath of the colours, in front of a fleur-de-lis Or, three lozenges conjoined in fess sable.'

After the shield and crest come the supporters, if there are any. It is a regrettable fact that there is a modern tendency for the officers of Arms, when granting supporters to say, 'on either side a (so and so)'. This is not only bad blazon, but it is bad grammar. What they mean is, 'on each side . . .'

To become master of the verbal art of blazon is to enter a new world of poetry and romance – it can be done without effort, but even should it demand hard work to acquire proficiency, it is highly rewarding.

99

100

CHAPTER SIX

Crests, Crowns and Flags

101

102

103

'ON a wreath of the colours . . .' is a kind of tocsin alerting the mind to receive the blazon of a crest, and only of a crest. A badge must not rest so (this is for England, not for Scotland) and a coat of arms cannot.

All crests are not, however, upon a wreath – how often in heraldry do we lay down a rule and quote exceptions in the same paragraph? A crest may stand upon a cap of maintenance, also called a cap of dignity, or a cap of estate, or a chapeau. In old heraldry it was reserved for the crest of a duke, but later it descended the social scale and could be used for commoners; today it is rarely (if ever) included in a new grant. This cap is the red lining of a crown or a coronet, and it carries the symbol of authority with it. At the State opening of Parliament it is the cap, not the crown, that is carried in procession.

It is lined with ermine, and turned up, or doubled, that is, the lower edge is rolled to display a strip of lining; this rolled portion is open behind, and terminates in two pointed tails. When the cap is depicted as the lining of a coronet, it sometimes has a tassel – generally of gold – in the centre top.

If the advent of a crest is not announced by 'on a . . .', it will be announced by 'out of . . .' Out of one of the heraldic crowns, or out of a ducal coronet, or out of a peer's coronet, in each case the crown, or the coronet, being named.

The crowns to which we refer as 'heraldic' are not of gold and precious gems; they do not exist except as heraldic drawing, and although they are said to have been used symbolically by the Romans to reward a victorious soldier, they did not become that soldier's permanent property; they were just fancy-dress for the occasion.

The mural crown is a circlet, tapering outward and upward, and it is crenelated at the top: five rising parts is strictly correct, but again, if four is more suited to the nature of the crest issuing from it, then make it four by all means. In addition to being embattled, the mural crown is ruled off into rectangular blocks and 'staggered' to look like masonry. It is blazoned as masoned, and the word 'sable', or else 'proper' may be (quite unnecessarily) added if the lines are black, but if they are to be of another colour then it must be stated. It is not only the mural crown; any object that appears in heraldry and is to be so represented, is described as masoned. The mural crown is, in modern times, generally related to civic heraldry: it will ensign the shield of a municipal corporation, in place of a helmet and crest. An ex-mayor, or ex-town clerk, receiving a grant of arms, may have his crest issuant of a mural crown, but it was originally military. The crown that ensigns the shield of the London County Council is simply a mural crown. Soon after receiving their grant they 'improved' upon it by substituting a continental crown, best described in English as a round tower with four ports and five bartizans. Recently they have 'improved' on the first 'improvement' by substituting a very ugly, non-existent shape which is neither British nor continental. This, sitting on a shield of 'improved' contours, seen from the distance, looks like a full-face portrait of a school-child suffering from mumps.

The antique crown, or eastern crown, or radiated crown, is a tapering circlet which terminates above in five rays, or sharp points. If to each point is added a mullet, it becomes crown-celestial.

There are two more spiked crowns. A circlet to the outer edge of which is attached by means of a nail or rivet, the head of which is shown in the drawing, seven long, slender rectangular pales with the top corners bevelled off each side is a crown-pallisado. The two outermost pales are chamfered at one angle only so as to give a profile view, because the crown, being circular, is carrying them away from the spectator's eye. Crown vallary finishes above with five vair bells and, again, the two outer ones are in profile.

The Naval crown is a circlet on which rests three sterns of sailing-ships – one at each end and one in the middle – and between them, in each space, a mast rigged with a square sail. Sometimes the order is reversed – three masts and two ships. This diversity does not seem to have, or ever to have had, a significance: it is either an alternative version of the same thing, so designed to conform to a crest, or else simply an error of drawing copied by an ignoramus from his predecessor, and ultimately accepted. This crown will be found in the arms of institutions and of persons connected with the great traffic of the oceans of the world.

A modern innovation is the Astral Crown – for organizations and men of the Air Force and Services. The full circlet would have on the upper edge four pairs of wings conjoined at the tips: in drawing there is seen one pair in the centre conjoined to the tip of a single wing at each side.

In Scotland the Lord Lyon King of Arms has, as recently as 1951, evolved a special crown to ensign the arms of a county council: it has five pales vert, alternated with four garbs Or. A Burgh has the mural crown, but if this ensigns the arms of an individual, the rule is that the person so honoured must be a distinguished soldier hence, in Scotland at least, the Roman idea is preserved in theory. There was, in 1917, a regrettable accident, when this crown was given to grace the armorial bearings of an architect!

The ducal coronet is not a duke's coronet. Like the foregoing heraldic crowns it has an existence in drawing only, but it differs from them in its being a coronet, although it is alternatively called an open crown.

It is represented as a circlet heightened with conventionalized strawberry leaves: one in the middle, and the inner half only of one at each end. The ducal coronet, or open crown, has a third name – a crest coronet: this is self-explanatory. In addition to acting as a crest bearer, it may appear as a charge on the field. 'Azure, three open crowns, Or,' the National Arms of Sweden.

We must now leave the land of make-believe, and handle precious metals and glittering gem-stones: from crowns and coronets that have an art-form existence only, we go to the Court

104

105

106

107

108

109

110

111

112

113

Jeweller and examine the objects that have being, that can be handled and, on appropriate occasions, placed upon the brow of one whose rank entitles him to thus distinguish himself.

The Crown Royal (or Crown Imperial) as depicted in heraldry represents the State Crown – not the St. Edward's Crown which is the official crown of England. It is a gold circlet enhanced with alternate crosses patty and fleurs-de-lis (four of each) heightened with two intersecting arches supporting an orb ensigned with a cross patty all encrusted with gems. The cap is always gules, although the actual cap of the State Crown is purple. In drawing, the central cross patty of the circlet is flanked on each side by a fleur-de-lis, these again by half only of a cross patty. The arch rising from these outer crosses passes over, but that from the central cross is foreshortened.

The State Crown used by King George V at the Delhi Durbar, in 1911, had double the number of crosses and fleurs-de-lis, and eight arches: that shown on the portrait of King Charles II is painted as having five arches visible, and the Continental Crown Royal is generally of five arches.

The coronet of the eldest son of the Sovereign (who does not become Prince of Wales until so created) is similar to the Crown Royal except that it is heightened by one arch only. The younger sons and daughters, and the brothers and sisters, of the Sovereign have the circlet enhanced with crosses patty and fleurs-de-lis, but they do not have the arches, and the Sovereign's grand-children, being offspring of princes, have the circlet enhanced with alternate crosses patty and strawberry leaves: those who are the offspring of princesses have alternate fleurs-de-lis and strawberry leaves. These coronets of the Royal family – in fact the State Crown itself – are not absolute: they may be altered by Royal warrant.

The Kings of Arms have their crowns which consist of a plain circlet of silver-gilt enhanced with sixteen (alternately eight tall and eight short) oak leaves (the Lord Lyon's crown has acanthus leaves, but there is no difference in appearance). The circlet is engraved with the words: *Miserere mei, Deus, secundum magnam misericordiam tuam,** which translates, 'Have mercy upon me, O God, according to thy loving kindness'.†

Under normal circumstances a King of Arms places the crown upon his brow once only, and not, as might be expected, at the time of his appointment. It is to be hoped that our present Garter King of Arms‡ never has the opportunity, and strange though it may seem, he will himself be first to endorse fervently that hope. The Kings of Arms assume their crowns at the actual moment of the Crowning of the Sovereign, hence, it is our prayer that both our present Garter and his ultimate successor or successors are enjoying a happy old age of retirement before there is another Coronation.

Notwithstanding that the crowns of the Kings of Arms are real objects, they are conventionalized in drawing, as also are the peerage coronets. Of the sixteen oak (or acanthus) leaves, nine are shown; five tall, and four short, those at each end in profile. If the cap is drawn it is gules, turned up ermine tasselled Or. The actual cap is of crimson satin, and is edged with ermine; it carries a gold tassel.

* *Psalmus L. Biblia Sacra juxta Vulgatae.*

† Psalms 51. Authorized Vervision. The numbering of Psalms in the *Hagiographa* (third division of the Hebrew Bible), and the renumbering in the Greek, the Latin, and the English translations do not coincide due to either the combining of two short psalms, or the division of one long one.

‡ Sir Anthony Richard Wagner, K.C.V.O., elevated from Richmond Herald on the retirement of Sir George Bellew, 1 August, 1961.

It is part of the glory of Her Majesty's Kingdom and Dominions that our aristocracy is not a caste – an intensely inbreeding minority into whose ranks none can penetrate.

The humble little boy, son of 'working class' parents, taking his seat today in an elementary school can, if he has the brains, the ambition and the ability to implement it, take his seat in the House of Lords in, say, forty years from now.

The Peerage of the United Kingdom is organized in five secular grades: Dukes, Marquises, Earls, Viscounts and Barons. The sixth grade of the Peerage, which is not secular, is the Archbishops and Bishops. Baronets, though considered as nobility do not rank as peers.

A duke's coronet is a circlet enhanced with eight strawberry leaves, five only of which appear in drawing: a marquis has alternate strawberry leaves and pearls: in drawing, a central strawberry leaf is between two pearls, and the outer leaves appear in profile. The coronet pearls are not the pearls from which necklaces are made: they are silver-gilt balls, an inch in diameter.

An earl's coronet has eight pearls but they do not rest on the circlet: they stand up from it on rods (called points) which look something like the 'horns' of a garden snail. Between the pearls, and down on the circlet, are strawberry leaves: in drawing, five pearl-topped points and four strawberry leaves appear. A viscount's coronet is enhanced with pearls only which rest on the upper edge of the circlet. In practice the minimum number is fourteen and the maximum sixteen: in drawing, seven only appear. A baron's (or lord's) coronet has six pearls only, four showing in drawing, but they are each two inches in diameter.

These peers' coronets generally ensign the shield, and the helmet of rank, bearing the crest, arises out of them.

The episcopal mitre has already been mentioned: although it is part of the ecclesiastical garb when archbishops and bishops wear it during sacred service, it nonetheless has the same status and symbolism as a coronet has when they attend the House of Lords. When ensigning their armorial bearings, the two purple ribbons fringed with gold, called *vittae infulae*, that depend from it, may be extended for their decorative value.

The Bishop of Durham, and he only, has a mitre rising out of a ducal coronet. This is to symbolize that *Dunelm* was once actually, and is now nominally, Count Palatine of Durham.

Mistakes in the etiquette of armorial display are seldom (if ever) made with the bearings of the ecclesiastical authorities,* but other public arms are frequently grossly misused, and private family arms suffer much from the ignorance of their owners.

We have already pointed out that over-emphasis of the crest causes shields to be forgotten, but very few armigers know that they have the right to fly, and ought to fly, a flag of their arms.

In England every person bearing arms should possess a banner: that is, a square flag having on it the contents of the shield, not the crest and supporters. That beloved flag known to the British public (and throughout the world) as 'The Royal Standard' is Her Majesty the Queen's Household banner. Where that flag flies, Her Majesty is.

Bodies corporate, particularly municipalities, misuse their arms: a flag they fly indeed with their entire achievement upon it. The present writer knows† of only one Town Hall where a correct armorial banner is flown correctly. That is Lambeth Town Hall (Brixton), London S.W.2.

The standard is a long, narrow, tapering flag, bearing the arms,

---

* None the less, ecclesiastical authorities can be the victims of astonishing armorial errors: see pages 84-85 .

† This does not imply that there are no others.

114

115

116

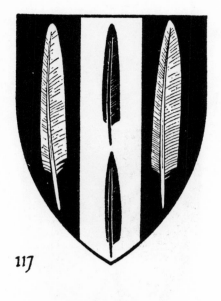

117

the crest and the badge. It may not be used by an armiger other than one who has received the grant of a badge.

That flags are misused by public bodies is a pity – that they are not used at all by most private persons is deplorable, but perhaps no flag is better than a wrong flag.

In Scotland the flying of armorial flags is under strict control. Every person who has matriculated arms is informed in the matter, and flags misused or misemblazoned would soon be destroyed by the Lord Lyon.

We can do no more here than simply mention flags, but the armorial flag and its use is an entrancing side-issue of heraldry that deserves much attention. *Armorial Standards*, by Robert Gayre, is not only a book full of knowledge on this subject, but it is readable and very brilliantly illustrated.

The 'Union Jack', as our national banner is miscalled, is a splendid example of combined national heraldic emblems, and were its blazon understood, it would not be flown inverted so often:

Azure, the crosses saltire of St. Andrew and St. Patrick, quarterly per saltire, counterchanged argent and gules, the latter fimbriated of the second, surmounted by the Cross of St. George of the third, fimbriated as the saltire.

A ship in harbour must fly its national flag from a mast set well forward. Her Majesty's ships wear the Union on this *Jack* staff – merchant ships difference with the Union within a bordure argent. See, moored in Thames river abaft Victoria Embankment, *Discovery*, *Wellington*, *Chrysanthemum*, and observe the flag that, during daylight hours, flys from the Jackstaff of each.

CHAPTER SEVEN

The Lion and the Mouse

118

119

THE animals that prowl and prance, that pose and dance upon the armorial field are different from those to be seen in the Zoo, or even in the jungle and on the wide prairie.

Even those that represent 'real' animals ought not to be drawn like photographs of stuffed dummies, and those that live only in legend, or in fairyland, should express strongly through their shape, their various attributes.

The most noble king of beasts, the lion, first claims the field. The herald-painter who had to depict him there when he entered upon the heraldic scene, kept before him the rule of filling the shield without overcrowding it. This he did by putting the lion's head in centre chief, his sinister hindpaw in centre base; his forepaws up and out, the dexter raised higher than the sinister, his dexter hindpaw in the flank, and his overlarge flashing, lashing, tufted tail filling the sinister flank.

This, at first, was the only position in which a lion appeared, hence he had no descriptive (adjectival) term, but was simply 'a lion'. Today he is generally called a lion rampant but, should the blazon give 'a lion', it is, even now, enough: a rampant lion is meant. Of course he (and all other beasts upon the field follow his example) faces dexter 'unless otherwise stated'.

Turned round to face the sinister he is a lion contourné, and he must change the position of his paws: he stands on the dexter hindpaw, the sinister forepaw being highest. A rampant lion is not, as the uninitiated think, representative of the lion fighting, or attacking, or springing; however, if there are two facing each other they are described as two lions combatant: lesser beasts in the same attitude are 'respecting each other.' (The lion, when meant to be in the act of springing, has both hindpaws on the ground, and is said to be salient.) Every lion, unless described as morné, which is very rare, is, without special mention of the fact, armed of its teeth and claws, langued of its tongue, and these are always gules, except in two circumstances: the first is when the field is gules, and the second, when the lion is himself of that tincture, but it is not even then left to chance; when not armed and langued gules a lion is so equipped azure.

It must be borne in mind that the lion is not a lioness, and this fact should be indicated, as indeed it should be with all other male animals on the heraldic field. In the nineteenth century animals were left unfinished, hence, strictly speaking, they should have been described as eviré.

120

 50

121

122

123

Although the lion normally ramps to the dexter, he does not necessarily always look in that direction (and the other beasts, of course, follow the example of their monarch). If he turns his head to face out of the shield he is rampant gardant (note there is no 'u' in this word): he is not on guard, but is simply looking. With his head turned completely round so as to gaze over his shoulder to the sinister, he is regardant.

The next position that the lion assumed was walking: his hind paws well apart, his dexter forepaw raised jauntily. Because he is walking he is passing, hence, blazoned as passant. He is often passant gardant, and with his head so, was described by the old French heralds (whom, it would seem, were the first to make his acquaintance) as a leopard. This, however, does not excuse the modern heraldists who continue to use unnecessarily the very misleading term – the same people spell *mullet* 'molet' – yet they insist, very inconsistently, on describing the Northern Irish quarter of the Royal Arms as charged with a gold harp with silver strings, exactly like a funeral furnisher's catalogue. The English quarter of the Royal Arms should be blazoned correctly by every loyal subject of Her Majesty who knows how to blazon: namely, 'gules, three lions passant-gardant in pale Or'. (Not three leopards, even though such a term was employed five hundred years ago.) For Scotland, as we know, 'the ruddy lion ramps in gold', hence, 'Or, a lion rampant within a double tressure flory-counter-fleury gules'.

A lion passant may be regardant, and may, if he feels so inclined, walk towards the sinister, when he becomes counter-passant. Should he pause in his walk and stand, all four paws planted firmly on the ground, he is statant. Should he then decide to squat on his haunches and rest, he is sejant: in an even more restful attitude – down on his chest, with paws stretched before him – he is couchant, and then, if satisfied that all is well, he may close both his eyes and his mouth, sink his chin on to his forepaws and take a nap, when he is described as dormant.

The lion normally flourishes his fine tail over his back, but there are times, particularly when he is statant, that he holds it out rigidly behind him. When he does this he is described 'with tail extended'. Often when couchant he will pass his tail down between his hindlegs, and flourish it over his flank. Any tail held thus downward causes the animal (including the lion) to be described as 'coward'.

Lions sometimes tie a figure-of-eight knot in their tail – generally when rampant – and receive the additional title of 'with tail knowed'.* A lion having two tails, both of full length, from the

* An alternative spelling is 'nowed'. The initial 'k' is preferable since the term refers to a knot. With the initial 'n' it may be confused with *nowy*.

124

125

base of the spine to the tufted tip, is 'double queued', but with one tail only emerging from the base of the spine, and this appendage, when of half length, branching into two, makes him 'queue-fourché'. With no tail at all he is 'a lion defamed'.

The King of Beasts appears on numerous occasions crowned. His normal crown is a ducal coronet but, if the blazon specifies, he may wear any crown – even the crown Royal. Another way in which he frequently wears his crown is about his neck, when he is blazoned as 'gorged with a ducal coronet.' Any heraldic beast having anything about his neck other than a strap and buckle collar is blazoned as gorged, but with an ordinary collar even the lordly lion may be described as collared, but is quite likely to be paid the compliment of 'gorged with a collar'.

A lion is sometimes drawn with a thin line of the field visible between his head and his body, and similar spaces between his body and his limbs: thus cut to pieces he is a lion tronnoné, or dismembered, or disjointed. A lion so mutilated becomes both ugly and undignified, but beauty of form is fully retained when parts of a lion appear as charges. First in frequency of application is the head. This may terminate at the neck in a straight line, making a lion's head couped; or it may be finished with three jagged curling points, when it is a lion's head erazed. (These two methods of removal – by cutting on the one hand, and by tearing on the other – may be applied to any part of any animal so treated.)

A lion's head, either couped or erazed, faces dexter unless blazoned as facing sinister (regardant) but it is never gardant. In the full-face position it can be neither couped nor erazed for it is drawn without the neck, and is named a lion's face. A lion severed at waist level is a demi-lion either couped or erazed, and close behind him will be that portion of his tail that would normally be level with the fore-half of his body. Thus halved he is either (and most frequently) a demi-lion rampant, or a demi-lion passant. He may be a demi-lion issuant in which case his waistline is in contact with something: a demi-lion issuant in base will appear to be cut off by the edge of the shield: 'a fess, and in chief a demi-lion issuant' will give him the appearance of walking on his hindlegs behind a wall represented by the fess. When a demi-lion is naissant he is rising out of, hence, 'a fess, and in chief a demi-lion naissant therefrom' would be drawn with the lion's waistline in the centre of the fess: he is rising from it, and is covering the middle part of the top line of the fess.

A lion's gambe (or jambe) is about two thirds of one of its forelegs; a lion's paw is severed at the 'wrist'. Both gambe and paw remain armed, and may be either couped or erazed.

According to an old legend, the two lions facing each other are combatant because there can be but one King on the field, but three are ignorant of each other's existence, each being king of his

131

132

133

own corner. More than three had to be kept apart by an ordinary, but since from very early times more than three did appear on the field without an ordinary to keep them apart, they were styled lioncels – meaning cubs.

When we are very young and we visit for the first time the Zoo, we are either amused to observe, or else puzzled by the fact that lions and tigers live in the cat-house because we think of the cat asleep on the hearth-rug at home, but in heraldry the tygre – for that is how he spells his name – does not show among the cats, but we will meet him (or her) in the land of make-believe.

The tiger proper, or the Bengal tiger, is a newcomer to the shield, and great cat though he is, is of little importance, but the heraldic small cat is quite at home among the old inhabitants. He is generally blazoned by the name 'catamount', which is a condensed form of cat-o'-the-mountains, a wild-cat, therefore a tough customer and should be drawn as such. A catamount éffarouché is in the rampant attitude, and herissonée he has his back up and his tail bristling. He is often sejant, but in any position he is likely to be gardant without the blazon saying so, and a catamount proper is tabby.

In modern times the domestic cat comes into heraldry in the same way as every conceivable kind of dog has appeared and been blazoned by the name of the breed, but there are three dogs only in old armorial bearings. The greyhound, so called; the mastiff, blazoned 'alant', and drawn with pricked ears, and, most common, the talbot, or huntsman's hound, drawn with drooping ears.

Wolves, demi-wolves and wolves' heads are common: so is the fox and the fox's head. The latter, full face, and without the neck shown, is blazoned as a fox's mask. A fox is often blazoned as a tod. When an animal's zoological description is also a surname, such as, for example, is Wolf, and Fox, the animal is very likely to appear in family arms. Any coat of arms (whether by use of animals or some other device) that makes a pun on its owner's name is termed a canting coat. Some of the old ones were very witty.

Among horned cattle the deer, because of his gracefulness, his speed and beauty, in addition to his having been the paramount animal of the chase in days of old, is first on the field in heraldry. The words stag, buck, hind and hart are inclined to be employed as if they were truly interchangeable, but stag ought to be reserved to mean a male red deer, buck a fallow deer, hind and hart a young deer without antlers.

All cattle are said to be unguled of their hooves and armed of their horns: the stag, however, is attired of his antlers. These are mentioned only when differing in colour from the animal, for example 'a stag argent, unguled Or, attired gules'. Special terms

134

135

are employed to indicate a stag's attitude: when another animal would be couchant the stag is lodged; walking, he is trippant; running, he is at speed; with both hind hooves on the ground, and the forelegs raised and flexed, he is springing (but might be called salient); standing with his head gardant, he is at gaze (but facing dexter, merely statant); with his head down to represent grazing, he is pascuant.

Demi-stags, and stags' heads, either couped or erazed, abound, but the most general position for a stag's head is gardant, when it is represented without the neck, and ·blazoned as caboshed.

Bulls, which, after stags, are the most usual cattle in the armorial field, must be drawn entire, or else an ox is indicated, and when the emasculated animal is required the blazon will say so – as in the civic arms of Oxford: 'barry-wavy in base [to represent water], an ox passant,' hence passing, that is, fording, making the canting composition Ox-ford. Bulls are often crowned, and may also be ringed, which refers to the leading ring through the nose. Cows seldom appear: calves are more common and a beautiful pun is to be found in calves for the family of Vaile.

Rams may be recognized by their circling horns, sheep are hornless and tailless,* lambs possess a tail, and have larger ears than their parents. The Paschal Lamb, or Holy Lamb, has a halo about its head, stands with its dexter foreleg flexed, and holds over its shoulder a cross-staff from which a pennon (pointed flag) is flotant. The fleece (or toison) may be either a lamb or a grown sheep. It is drawn as though it were alive, and hanging by a belt round its middle, but it represents a sheepskin with the wool attached.

The goat, an objective, adventurous fellow, has long curved horns, and when rampant is blazoned as clymant. The domestic hog is paid the compliment of being termed a boar, and the wild boar answers to the name sanglier. Both the boar and the sanglier have tushes, or tusks, protruding from the lower jaw; each has a curled tail terminating in a tuft. Pig's heads, either couped or erazed but generally the former, may be severed immediately behind the ears, or they may retain the neck: the former is couped close; the latter, couped at the neck. In British heraldry we do not make coats of arms of hams, but we are not without eggs.

Horses one would expect in heraldry, for was it not the armoured warrior who developed the painted shield, the embroidered surcoat, and the armorial horse-trapper? There are, indeed, numerous examples of horse and rider armed cap-à-pie (from head to foot), but horses often appear without a rider. A

* Sheep acting as supporters may be given a tail.

136

137

138

139

140

141

142

143

144

145

146

147

148

149

horse comparisoned has, over his back, a saddle cloth: comparisoned and furnished, adds a saddle and a bridle. He may, too,
be simply saddled, or bridled, and the draught-horse, often
harnessed, is as popular as the more slender animal.

When standing, the horse is described as upright; when running,
either as courant, or as trotting – sometimes, if the speed is
increased to a gallop, he is said to be in full career. A horse rampant is quite definitely rampant – all four limbs assume the same
position as those of any other rampant animal: but when the
horse has both his hind-hooves on the ground, though they are
spaced wide apart, the horse is forcene, or rearing, or salient.
Horses are often wrongly drawn and wrongly blazoned, it being
supposed that forcene is another term for rampant. A young
horse is a colt, which is male. He is crined of his mane and his
tail: the hair should be generously drawn, long and curling.
Demi-horses are common as crests, and horses' heads, more
often couped than erazed, are correctly blazoned as nags' heads.

This, a familiar public-house sign, reminds one of the famous
house that gave its name to a whole area of south-east London,
namely, the Elephant and Castle. In heraldry nearly every elephant carries an embattled round tower on his back. There are
no demi-elephants, but heads, often erazed, are to be met with,
and their tusks sometimes are seen in crests.

Bears are more common than elephants. The bear is generally
sejant erect – begging for buns as it were – but he is often muzzled
as well. Bears' heads may be couped close or couped at the neck.
The other portions of his anatomy that appear alone are his paws.

Among the small animals must be mentioned both the hare
and the rabbit, called coney; and the hedgehog called either
herisson (from Old French) or urcheon (from Old English). The
ermine, the stoat and the weasel are treated in heraldry as though
they were three separate creatures: in nature it is but three names
for the same creature. The badger has two names: either the
brock, or the grey: squirrels with their bushy tails are generally
sejant: the mole, called moldiwarp, is likely to be passant.
Heraldry is not without rats and mice and bats, and this last
creature leads from quadrupeds to birds.

151

152

150

153

CHAPTER EIGHT

Feather, Fin and Fly

154

155

'AGAIN their ravening eagle rose' and we observe the fierce and mighty bird in the forefront of Continental heraldry, but so striking a creature, employed for symbolic display by the Romans, cannot be the exclusive property of any person or of any nation. Hence we find many eagles in English armory. The most important attitude that he assumes is what is termed displayed: he spreads his mighty pinions wide, presents himself affronté, expands his huge talons, and, with tongue protruding, gazes fixedly to the dexter. (Should he look in the opposite direction he may be called regardant, but he ought to be called recursant.*)

The wings of an eagle displayed may have their tips tucked into the top corners of the shield, or they may turn downward reaching often to his claws: if the former is required, the blazon ought to describe the eagle displayed as 'with wings elevated', if the latter, 'with wings inverted', but seldom are these wing-positions mentioned: it is assumed that the elevated attitude is British, and the inverted Continental, however, there is no rule – many British eagles invert their wings. A very familiar example of an eagle with wings inverted is that of Barclays Bank, which is also charged on the breast, and on each wing, with an open crown.

It is only birds of prey that should be blazoned as displayed – all others ought to be called disclosed when in the same position, but this rule is very often violated. In a like manner, only a bird of prey ought to be described as armed of its beak and claws: others should be 'beaked and membered' (or legged).

Care must be taken not to confuse the terms 'an eagle displayed' and 'an eagle with wings displayed'. In the former position we are given a view of the bird in flight, as though pouncing on his prey, in the latter he is perched, faces dexter, and has his wings half raised as if about to take flight. This attitude may be assumed by any bird, as may be the complete raising of the wings so that they meet over the bird's back, thus altering the blazon to 'with wings addorsed'.

Any winged creature, bird, insect or hybrid out of legend, is described as 'volant' when represented as on the wing, and as 'close' when resting with the wings closed. Eagles' heads, either couped or erazed, and legs, generally erazed from the body, and described as erazed à la quise, make interesting charges: a leg

* The idea that an eagle recursant is a 'difference' to indicate illegitimacy is without any foundation: it is in the category of 'bar-sinister'.

57

severed below the thigh – always couped – is blazoned as an eagle's claw. A bird of prey's claw may be called its pounce.

The hawk has been a favourite device since the days when every gentleman was a falconer. The bird has numerous names – hawk falcon, goshawk, hobby, girfauk, merlion, and even puttock is not unknown although, strictly, it should be applied only to the kite, or to the buzzard.

The hawk rode perched upon the falconer's wrist, hence, his common attitude is perched and close, but he is often, also, rising, or surgerant; and sometimes standing on another bird and described as 'preying upon', or as 'trussing'.

In order to prevent the hawk starting in pursuit at his own discretion, he was carried blindfolded. This is blazoned as 'hooded', and drawn as though he was wearing a little head-scarf, neatly tied under his chin.

The hawk's head and beak are rounder than those features in an eagle, hence no confusion occurs between an eagle's head when used as a charge, and that of a hawk so employed, but the claws of the two birds are the same, and the falcon's, when used as a separate charge, can be distinguished only by its bell.

All falcons, whether the blazon mentions it or not, carry a spherical bell (like that on a baby's rattle), secured to the claw by a strap; and this itself may have rings attached to the ends. The straps are the jesses, the rings the vervells, so a hawk is sometimes blazoned as belled jessed and vervelled. This is usually done only when the bells, the straps and the rings are of different colours. Double belled, or belled on both legs, speaks for itself. The bells alone may appear as charges.*

Another bird of great importance – perhaps more frequent in its appearances than any other – is the heraldic swallow, named the martlet. A martlet is always close, and in place of claws he has little stumps. When on the wing, the swallow is not called a martlet, but is simply a swallow volant, sometimes, though not often, the French term is used – a hirondelle.

The heraldic dove is kept hard at work, too. He is distinguished by having on the back of the head a tuft, and is membered either proper or gules, the former being pink (pale gules). When perched the dove often carries in his beak a twig, and the blazon will specify its nature.

Another old inhabitant of the field is the Cornish chough (chuff) who is always sable, beaked and membered gules. Three Cornish choughs appear in the civic arms of Canterbury because the bird's name in old heraldry is 'beckit'.

The fighting cock is fairly common. He is described as armed of his beak, claws and spurs; crested of his comb; and may be either jelloped, or wattled, but often these appendages are absent. Ducks appear by various names including shoveller, and sheldrake; swans make most beautiful devices, and are often gorged with a coronet: the lapwing, the peewit and the plover are three names for one bird: a partridge is sometimes blazoned as a gregor, a goose as a bernicle. The wise old owl remains gardant no matter how he is orientated: the parrot, vert, beaked and membered gules, or else proper which is the same, is called either a popinjay or a papegay: the ostrich, having fulsome tail-feathers and tiny wings, is further distinguished by generally holding in the beak an article of ironmongery; the heron, who may be blazoned herne, is drawn with a tufted head, and holds in his beak an eel: the stork holds a snake, but is not tufted, and is, of course, hunchbacked. The crane is tufted, but there will be no confusion, for a crane stands upon the sinister claw, holding in the dexter, which is flexed, a piece of rock. He is blazoned as

156

157

158

* But see the note on p. 82.

159

160

161

'a crane in his vigilance'. The piece of rock, when appearing alone, is a crane's vigilance.

Other birds have similar descriptive titles: the 'peacock in his pride' stands affrontée and has his fan (tail) spread; and the 'pelican in her piety' is perched on a nest where, surrounded by her young, she wounds her breast, which is gouttée de sang, and feeds them on her blood. When the young are not present she is 'a pelican vulning herself', but is sometimes mis-blazoned.

In addition to heads and legs, wings occur as separate charges: nearly always it is a single wing, described as a demi-vol without specifying the bird. Unless blazoned as inverted, the wing-tip is chiefward. A pair of wings is called 'a hawk's lure', or 'two wings conjoined in leure', and the tips are baseward.

Feathers occur in their own right, simply as feathers, but sometimes the quill is coloured, and described as penned of the colour, and the whole feather may be called a pen.

When feathers are employed as crests they are generally in a plume of several, as a rule, an odd number, up to five, after which the term a panache of so many feathers may be applied. When one row of feathers appears behind and above another, each 'height' being smaller till it finishes in one only at the top, it may be called a pyramid of feathers.

The pelican in her piety functioned as a symbol of motherhood, and of self-sacrifice, long before heraldry was evolved. It ought not to be assumed, however, that heraldry is merely a preserving fluid in which old ideas may be crystallized: it is a living, organic force, expressing its vitality by eliminating outworn tissue, and manifesting itself in new forms. We see, in our own time, the helmet of rank, for example, passing away; and those of us who are conversant with current trends rejoice to learn of the incorporation of new figures. Among these may be mentioned the fish-eagle of Rhodesia, which makes its appearance in several grants to African corporations. There is, also, the manilla, a horse-shoe shaped object representing the ancient coinage of the Gold Coast (Ghana).

This healthy tendency to revise and reform has never been absent: for example, the flying-fish, which few people before the days of Elizabeth I had actually seen, was drawn as a fish equipped with the long tapering feathered wings of a swallow. Sir Francis Drake, intrigued by the creatures, observed them very carefully, and he brought home with him an accurate description. From that time the flying-fish in heraldry has been drawn with gauze-like wings: still long and tapering, but by no means those of a bird.

A sea-creature figured in arms, and one whose prehistory as a symbol antedates the Christian era, is the dolphin. The heraldic dolphin, in common with other creatures, is drawn with exaggerated curves and characteristics, but they are clearly sea-mammals. As a rule they lie fess-wise, and are embowed, that is, curved in a shallow S shape, the head to the dexter, down, the tail up. Proceeding to the sinister, they are counter-embowed, and if stretched out they are said to be extended.

There is barely a fresh-water, or a sea-fish that does not figure in arms, in fact there is a book* that deals exclusively with the subject, but here we can mention only those of the greatest importance, or frequency of occurrence.

When any fish (and it applies also to the dolphin) is fess-wise, head to the dexter, it is naiant; head to sinister, counter-naiant. A fish in pale with its head in chief is hauriant; in pale with the head in base, urinant. Hauriant in bend, and urinant in bend are terms that need no gloss.

The river pike, drawn with a fierce, doglike head, is called a Lucie (or Lucy) or a gad (or ged) occasionally even a jack, and he generally appears in a canting setting.

* Thos. Moule, *Heraldry of Fish.*

Fish often go in pairs (like kippers), when hauriant with ventral surface to ventral surface they are respecting each other: with dorsal surface to dorsal surface they are addorsed.

Salmon, are of course, important, but not more so than is the humble herring: in fact, if the blazon gives simply 'a fish', then the herring is intended. The cod, too, is very important, and he enters heraldry in two forms: normally alive, like any other fish in the field; but also decapitated, split open, and salted he is the stockfish – once an item of British export – and is depicted looking like a modern finnan-haddock.

Conger eels are generally represented by their head only, but the ordinary edible small eel, sometimes blazoned as a grig is, as a rule, quite whole. He may be represented as either afloat or ashore, free, or gripped in a mailed fist; he writhes in the heron's beak, and lined up in a row he peeps over the rim of a cooking-pot.

Whelks and escallops are represented by their empty shells: the former for a canting charge (Wilkinson, Shelley), the latter symbolic, being the insignae of St. James the Great, Patron of Pilgrims. Crabs and crayfish, the latter sometimes styled crevice, one may assume to be alive when they put in an appearance, but the lobster is very dead. His claw is all that comes into heraldry and even that is conventionalized in drawing to look like a cracked wooden spoon.

In recent times, and arising out of the Englishman's adventurous enterprise and his pioneering spirit, creatures hitherto unknown have come into arms: among them will be found the gigantic tropical reptiles; alligators and crocodiles, who are probably held in contempt by our very own indigenous old reptilian inhabitants, the frogs and the toads. The former answer to the name powerts, the latter to crapawdys. The newt, called either aske, or swift, appears in canting settings, and when proper he is vert. This applies, too, when he is blazoned as effert, a term that may cover all lizardlike creatures. A tortoise displayed turgiant in fess, is passant, but we look down upon him, seeing his four limbs, his head and his tail. When he is laboriously proceeding from base to chief he is less grandly blazoned: the one word 'erect' is used.

'Now the serpent was more subtil than any beast of the field,' and he is more supple than any beast on it, for notwithstanding the heraldic contortions and contours of most beasts they do not tie themselves into figure of eight knots, and that the serpent very often does: it is, in fact, his favourite heraldic pastime. A serpent (or a snake) knowed has his head and tail emerging from the tangle inclined upward. If they are to point downward he is knowed-reversed: at least, that is as it should be, but many incline their extremes in whatever direction the artist sees fitting. A snake involved is one who, making himself into an annulet, takes his tail into his mouth. Extended in fess he is gliding or glissant; in pale he is erect; if, however, he raises his length in a series of humps he is, if in fess, glissant-wavy; and in pale ondoyant. One snake, winding round a stick, with head in chief, makes a composition called the rod of Aesculapius: when two serpents wind in opposite directions, and the rod itself is winged, the entire composition is the caduceus, or the rod of Hermes or of Mercury. These rod and snake compounds are symbolic of healing and appear in arms of doctors, and medical institutions. 'How,' the reader must be thinking, 'can one distinguish between a snake and an eel?' – Easily! The snake's mouth is open; his fangs long, curved and dangerous looking, his forked tongue extended.

One could, by the use of another quotation from the Old Testament, introduce our next creature – the bee. Volant, and

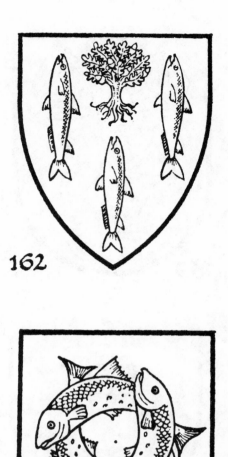

162

163

164

165

viewed from above as it were, they are blazoned as 'volant in arrière'. 'Promiscuously volant,' or 'diversely volant,' or 'sans nombre' they appear in a group generally about a hive. Industrial magnates, taking up a grant, like bees, the symbol of industriousness, as well as bezants – which are the outcome of it, so if the bee will not grace their field he may become a crest – no longer volant, but standing, with wings elevated.

Butterflies, too, are volant in arrière, the four wings being very distinct, but seldom are they bright with colour. The best thing about them is their heraldic title, papillon. The harvest fly has two wings only, but they cover the area of papillon's four, and the legs are visible. The gad-fly, gad-bee, or brimsey has four wings but narrow, backward inclined, and inconspicuous.

The grasshopper is famous as a device all over the civilized world because it is the cognizance of Sir Thomas Gresham, and graces the pinnacle of London's Royal Exchange. It is sometimes blazoned as a cicada which is actually the name of a quite different insect. There are but few examples of the grasshopper, but comparatively many of the humble ant, blazoned as emmet, and often in large numbers on a little hill.

*   *   *

Note: For centuries there has been lively controversy on the use of the term 'belled and jessed'. It was contended by some that the word 'jessed' was redundant since the bird could not be 'belled' were it not 'jessed'. The present writer held the opinion that the double description was needed only when the bells and the jesses were of different colours.

A falcon 'belled and jessed' appeared as crest in the achievement of Col. Geoffrey A. Puttock, devised by Portcullis Pursuivant late in 1961, and the matter was investigated by Garter King of Arms who discovered that not one strap was involved, but two. The bell-thong is automatic, and must always accompany the bell: the jess, however, is an attachment to which the leash was affixed. Col. Puttock's Patent (1962) is the first in which this dualism is depicted and is therefore of historical importance. (See blazon and illustration No. 109.)

CHAPTER NINE

Dragons, Monsters and Men

THE fictitious creatures of heraldry either trip daintily upon the ever sunny fields of fairyland, or they snort and bellow from the backwoods of nightmare. All the major ones have a meaning and a history, sometimes much longer than that of heraldry itself, but neither of these interesting aspects of fictitious animals can be dealt with here, nor is it possible to parade the whole of the crazy circus – only those creatures that make frequent appearances will be briefly introduced.

The best known of all fictitious creatures is the Unicorn. Not everyone who knows a unicorn is quite sure that it is fictitious: further, most people, asked to describe it, would say it is a horse with a spiral horn on its forehead. They are not to blame for this ignorance. It is often so drawn – even when acting as a supporter of the Royal Arms.

The unicorn is in fact based on a goat, has cloven hooves, and a beard. He may be blazoned either as rampant or clymant, and it should be observed that he has an heraldic lion's tail.

Sometimes 'real' animals are 'improved': a lion, for example, may be given two heads, or one head may be attached to two, or even three, bodies. A lion bicorporate and a lion tricorporate being the description employed.

A lion with a pair of wings, either sejant or statant, should be described as a winged lion, not as 'The Lion of St. Mark'. That term applies strictly only to a winged lion statant, resting its dexter forepaw on an open book, and having about the head a halo.

A lion having the face of a man is often called simply a man-lion, seldom by his own name, a lympago: a lion who, from the waist downward, becomes a fish and who, to strengthen the shape-change, has webbed forepaws, is nearly always called by his own name, a morse; sometimes, however, a 'sea-lion'. His usual attitude is facing dexter, his tail curled under him and carried away to the sinister. Thus he is sejant, but he may also be naiant and, when emerging from water, assurgeant.

A sea-dog is a talbot with webbed paws and with the dorsal fin starting at the neck running into a broad tail like that of a beaver. The sea-horse may be either crined or finned, as may be the sea-stag.

A winged horse is called Pegasus; a winged stag, based on the same plan, has no special name. The stallion is sometimes

166

167

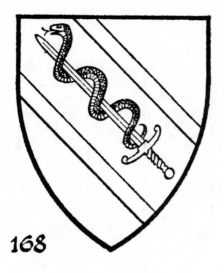

168

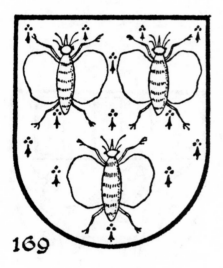

169

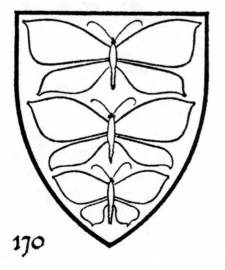

170

combined with the human form by having, in place of the horse's neck and head, the trunk, head and arms of a man. His name is Centaur, but given a bow and arrows he becomes Sagittarius.

There are several combinations of a bird and a woman. The harpy is a vulture with a woman's head and breast, the siren is a woman to the pelvis, but has the legs and webbed feet of a sea-bird as well as, from the shoulder, a pair of long, narrow wings.

The heraldic tygre has a lion's tail, body and limbs, but it has a longer neck than a lion has, and this sprouts a horse's mane. The head is that of a wolf, but the upper jaw has, in place of nostrils, a long, corkscrew-like horn. If in place of paws we put cloven hooves, and add to the head a pair of straight horns with a jagged underside, the animal is an heraldic antelope. A further metamorphosis takes place if we cut the tail off short, and give curved horns in place of straight ones. This, the yale, is very uncommon, but as one of The Queen's Beasts which, moulded in plaster, were stood in a picturesque row on guard outside Westminster Abbey Annexe, he attracted more than his fair share of attention, and far too much Press publicity, at the time of Her Majesty's Coronation, and this unwarranted notoriety has been kept alive by the enterprising manufacturers of various useless fancy goods – 'A Present from London'.

Another curious composite creature is the enfield. An old writer says he has 'the head of a fox, the chest of a greyhound, the talons of an eagle and the hindlegs and tail of a wolf'. We cannot improve on that.

One must include the double-headed, or Imperial Eagle, but observe that the American eagle is content to represent, with its one head only, a powerful nation. A demi-eagle, tufted, generally argent, but sometimes Or, is the Phoenix. She is always issuant of flames of fire proper, for the legend surrounding her is that when she became elderly and tired she built a pyramid of spice-wood, ignited it by fanning with her wings, and then, plunging into it, arose rejuvenated from the embers.

Another creature of the fire is the salamander, a fictitious lizard that lives in the flames, hence he, too, is always accompanied by his chosen element and he is often blazoned as 'a salamander in the fire'.

St. George fought with and conquered a dragon and, in fairy-story, many a fair maiden has been rescued from a malicious dragon by a brave knight; however, all dragons are not ill-natured; the most important dragon in heraldry is the griffin (or gryphon) who is all virtue. She (for all griffins are ladies) is keen of eye and quick of ear, vigilant and faithful. Even in her shape she is not ugly – not scaley and spikey – her hindquarters are those of a lion (or rather, lioness), her forequarters and wings those of an eagle, but she has a pair of ears attached to her head. She generally assumes the rampant attitude, is blazoned as segreant, and may be further described as armed, or as beaked and forelegged. The wings, seldom mentioned in blazon, are addorsed. Demi-griffins are common, so are griffins' heads, and were it not for the ears, these parts would be indistinguishable from the corresponding parts of an eagle.

A male griffin is without wings, and he exudes rays from each joint. Either the male or the female may at times snort fire and smoke from the nostrils. Incensed is the correct term. Fumant, which is often applied, really is more suited to forges, furnaces and kilns. The griffin is a very old form of fictitious creature, but the opinicus that is derived from it does not appear before the sixteenth century. It has an eagle's head, with ears; its neck, longer than that of a griffin, may be either feathered or scaled; all four limbs are those of a lion, but the tail is cut short. The wings are not feathered, as a bird's are, but are membraneous, as are those of a bat.

The opinicus was probably suggested by the wyvern (the latter word is Old English for viper) which has large membraneous wings, but its head is doglike with a snaggy hook rising from the snout. The neck and chest are birdlike in build but are covered with large, overlapping scales, and from the chest downward it tapers away to end in a barbed (arrowlike) tail. It usually rests upon this extremity, supporting itself in bend by its two eagle's legs. Its snakelike character is indicated by its tongue which, always protruding, is also barbed.

The wyvern becomes the dragon (pictured as being slaughtered by St. George) when it has four scaly legs, and numerous spikes, spines and snags extending from its scales. Another creature that can be classified as a form of dragon is the cockatrice. In appearance it is a wyvern with a cock's head. The young of a cockatrice differ from their parent by having, at the end of the tail, a dragon's head. This creature may be blazoned as an amphisian cockatrice, but is far more likely to appear as a basilisk.

Now we are bewitched in the horrid land of dragons, and there seems to be no escape, but the fairy mermaid comes to our aid and leads us back to the world of men. She has a lovely face, and is crined of her long golden hair, in which she takes great pride. In her dexter hand she holds her mirror, blazoned often as her peering glass, and in her sinister hand she holds her comb. She generally wears a girdle of seaweed, and her fishlike extremity is slender and delicately fashioned. Sometimes she is impersonated by a rather vulgar second cousin of hers, who invariably overdoes it by wearing two tails. Her name is Melusine. The mermaid's consort is King of the Ocean, Neptune, or Triton: he wears an open crown, sometimes an Eastern crown, is bearded, and carries his trident before him, held in bend sinister.

Mermaids and mermen have been known to come ashore and live in the hollow hills with the land-fairies. They have, from time to time, been seen and, more frequently, heard singing their plaintive wordless sad song that men mistake for the music of the spheres on their long tracks through space, or for the harps and hymns of the celestial choir.

Most of the angels who appear in heraldry are supporters, far too occupied to sing or strum the harp. They are, as a rule, female angels, who stand full face, and have the long golden hair of the mermaid. Unlike these little sea-fairies, angels are not preoccupied with their personal appearance and they are always dressed; 'habited', as the blazon puts it, in a long-robe, as the blazon again puts it, which may be tied with a girdle of cord about the waist, when 'close-girt' is added to the description. Angels' wings are constructed on the long, narrow side, are feathered and white, and they remain close and inverted. Their hands, when not occupied with some pious task – even so humble as that of holding up a shield, are 'conjoined and elevated upon the breast'.

Cherubs, consisting of a chubby infant's head borne on a pair of wings, are often to be met with; and seraphs, the same head, but set in a starlike cluster of six wings, are not unknown.

There are very many saints to be found in heraldry, often in civic arms, for old cities nearly always had the representation of their patron saint in their official seal from the design of which the arms were quite often composed. Most saints can be identified by the symbol of their acts: a hind pierced by an arrow for St. Giles, tongs for St. Dunstan, keys for St. Peter; or, if they were martyrs as well as saints, by the implement of their martyrdom: the grid for St. Lawrence, the spiked wheel for St. Catherine.

171

172

173

Conventionalized human figures symbolic of virtue, and of other ethical ideas are to be met: Justice, blindfold holding scales, is typical – who could fail to recognize her? A king, or a bishop will be known by the symbol of his office; conspicuous in the hands of the former the orb (called a mound) and sceptre, and on his head a crown: the latter will hold the pastoral staff, and wear the mitre. Soldiers and sailors, miners and other craftsmen have been mentioned in relation to their usual function of supporters, and fulfilling that task, too, will be found saracens, savages and blackamoors. These last are inclined to be expressed by their heads alone (always couped) and they occur frequently on the field. Both saracens and savages belong to the white race and are bearded. Saracens are habited, and wreathed with foliage about the temples: savages are naked and are wreathed about both the temples and the loins. Blackamoors, drawn intensely negroid, often have the neck enwrapped, entwined or entwisted with a serpent.

It is not only the human head that appears among charges – the leg and, far more often, the arm do. The latter is generally couped at the shoulder and, unless otherwise stated, naked. When 'otherwise stated' it may be either habited or vested, or else clad in armour and blazoned as vambraced. Arms are usually flexed at the elbow and described as embowed but the blazon must state whether it is a dexter or a sinister arm. Embowed erect, that is, palewise, the elbow is to the dexter, and the hand, clenched unless otherwise stated, is to the sinister. An arm vambraced terminates in a gauntlet. Arms couped at the elbow are uncommon, but couped between the elbow and the wrist and blazoned as 'a cubitt arm' one meets many. When an arm is vested, it may be cuffed of another colour, but the hand remains proper. In old heraldry they sometimes employed the word 'car'* for flesh colour. If the hand is to be of an heraldic colour it is said to be gloved: for example, 'a cubitt arm vested gules, cuffed azure, gloved sable'.

Hands, generally couped at the wrist, are seldom anything other than erect, and apaumé, that is, the fingers are in chief, and the palm of the hand is visible. A dexter-hand has the thumb towards the sinister, hence, which hand is intended must be stated.

Thigh-bones and shin-bones appear fairly often – so does the skull blazoned as a death's head, but the only internal organ to have found its way into heraldry is the heart. Even doctor's coats of arms do not have livers and stomachs and kidneys as charges. Hearts are sometimes crowned, and at other times they are ensigned with flames of fire proper, but they are nearly always gules, because a heart proper is gules.

* 'Car' was really an abbreviation: one also finds it expanded to both 'carnat' and 'carnation'. The meaning is, of course, either 'incarnadine', or 'incarnate'.

CHAPTER TEN

Forest to Wreath of Fame

'. . . THE murmuring pines and the hemlocks, bearded with moss, and in garments green, indistinct in the twilight, stand like Druids of old, with voices sad and prophetic,' for which depressing attitude no one can blame them: 'the forest primeval' thus introduced by Longfellow is not aiming to be heraldic, hence, vigorous and inspiring.

The animals that inhabit the heraldic field would not do to illustrate a manual of zoology; it is, however, a hardly hideable fact that most of the vegetation depicted in arms would go quite well in a book on botany. More than ordinary artistic ability is demanded to give the beasts their bounce and beauty; it calls for nothing short of genius to draw an oak-tree so as to suggest animation and force without distortion of form.

Every tree in the heraldic forest that is not specified, but is blazoned simply as 'a tree', is assumed to be an oak, which is of first importance since Europe was once clothed in oak forest, and early man ate and enjoyed the fruit thereof – 'acorns were good till bread was found' said Juvenal. What is more, the English Navy was built of English Oak.

174

Although there is as wide a divergence in the morphology of trees as in that of, say, quadrupeds, fewer people, and particularly those constituting the urban populations, are aware of it, hence, in heraldry the leaves are drawn as of huge dimensions in relation to the entire tree. An oak-tree proper (or of either metal or any tincture) will have a dozen or twenty leaves only to make up the whole 'head'. In this way the shape of the leaf is a visible indicator of the nature of the tree.

Any tree bearing its fruit may be blazoned as 'fructed', but the oak has a specialized term, namely, acorned. In nature, acorns are smaller than the leaves; in heraldry, larger.

The earth is no longer populated by giants who wear oak-trees in their buttonholes, therefore the heraldic tree is assumed to be rooted, and is blazoned as issuant – for example, 'on a chief, three oak-trees issuant' means that the foot of each trunk is in contact with the base-line of the chief; however, many trees are issuant of (or on, or from) a mount. Sometimes there will be added, quite redundantly, after 'mount', the further description, 'in base vert'.

A mount, which is a little hillock, is always, unless otherwise stated, in base, and likewise, vert. A mount may be drawn

66

175

176

177

simply as a rising semicircle, but the herald-painter who is an artist will give it character by making it a little rugged in its contour, out of balance slightly, and spangled with daisies.

When a number of trees are to stand in juxtaposition, the group may be described as a hirst (or hurst) of so many trees. As many English surnames are derived from place-names, and as many English places have names that end in *hurst*, it will be seen that such groups sough to the whisper of the punning wind.

Trees may be either felled, or torn from the earth by their roots. Any fool with an axe has freedom to commit murder on a tree – particularly if he wishes to park the car in what was the front garden: none of these heroes of the hack-it-down breed have strength to pull even a sapling up by the roots. This feat is left to the tough-guys of psuedo-Canadian lumberjack fiction, and the learned Officers of Arms.

A tree in its entirety with roots exposed is blazoned as eradicated, and even when it is eradicated proper, the exposed roots are not, they are invariably conventionalized into an asymmetrical pattern.

The pine parades second to the oak, and may be described as any one of the varieties of *genus pinus*, but it is likely to be drawn as a typical Christmas-tree with drooping branches. When fructed, the pine-cones appear disproportionately large. When standing in their own right they may be blazoned as pineapples, which seems strange, but is no stranger than the Frenchman's 'apple of the earth' for an ordinary potato.

Trees do not have heraldic names, though some of them answer to more than one: the willow may be called salix or osier; the mountain-ash, rowan: but apple-trees, pear-trees, cherry-trees, walnut-trees, palm-trees and coconut-trees, orange-trees and lemon-trees are marked in plain figures, as the shop-keepers say.

When a tree has been felled, the stump left in the ground is called the stock, and it may be either issuant or eradicated. The trunk, blazoned as 'the log of a tree', is generally in fess, and very often is sprouting – that is, a living twig with a leaf or two, springs from it.

Branches are either couped (or truncated) or else slipped. The former indicates that the limb has been sawn off, and is drawn with a flat end, the latter that it has been torn off and the end is an elongated oval. Branches are assumed to be living, and are clothed in foliage unless blazoned as withered, starved or blasted, when they will have twigs, but not leaves: a branch lopped has the points of the twigs cut off.

A twig, with its leaves (even fructed), is generally blazoned as a slip: it may, however, be called a sprig, but this term is inclined to be reserved for the olive. 'And for his crest, upon a wreath of the colours, a dove proper holding in the beak a sprig of olive.'

Any leaf, unless more than averagely ill-drawn, will be easily recognizable, even by a town dweller. Who would not know an oak-leaf, or a maple-leaf, a strawberry-leaf or a fig-leaf? The normal position for a leaf, which will have the stalk intact, is with the tip towards the chief. The veins in a leaf are invariably depicted, and if they are to be distinctive, the leaf is blazoned as nerved: for example, 'an oak-leaf Or nerved gules': 'a maple-leaf proper nerved sable'. When leaves are secondary, they should blend in with the design, but do so modestly: they take this sub-ordinate role when a fruit is blazoned as slipped and leaved.

'Fruit' can be a broad term. (Sometimes a super-shiny chromium-plated motor-car is the fruit of vulgarity.) As a rule we accept it in the narrow sense – apples and pears, cherries and plums, bananas and pineapples: this last not the pine-cone which is blazoned pineapple, but the fruit of the plant *ananassa sativa*, hence, blazoned as 'ananas'.

The apple of Granada, more frequently blazoned by its prosaic greengrocer's name, pomegranate, was brought into English heraldry by Catharine of Aragon. It is, as a rule, blazoned proper, and is drawn slipped and leaved, and with a strip of skin cut away to reveal the grains (seeds) that fill the interior. It will be drawn in the same way when of one of the tinctures or the metals, but it will then be 'seeded proper', which is gules.

Apples and pears, nearly always slipped and leaved, are pendant; that is, hanging as in nature before they are gathered, unless blazoned as inverted, or fess-wise. Bunches of grapes inverted are described as erect.

Much of the fruit in arms is there for canting reasons: 'argent, three apples slipped and leaved proper in chief', for the name of Appleton is very obvious: pears for the name Perry do not keep one guessing for long, but pears for the name Warden will suggest nothing to the man who has never heard of Warden pears.

Oranges and lemons, peas and beans and hops and peppers, and in fact all edible fruits known, including nuts – walnuts for Waller – as well as some not so edible, are of fairly frequent occurrence.

Chief among the non-edible nuts is of course the acorn which one may expect to meet slipped and leaved. Root crops are not ignored: in British heraldry the leek has pride of place but on the Continent parsnips, turnips and carrots are accepted as reasonable and dignified charges.

Leaving the vineyards and orchards we find, in farm and field, that 'those who husbanded the golden grain, and those who flung it to the winds like rain' also tied it up into sheaves. That was before farming was done on the conveyor-belt system. Heraldic sheaves of grain are called garbs, but unless wheat is intended, the nature of the grain must be added, as a 'garb of barley', 'a garb of oats', or 'two garbs of rye in saltire'. A garb is always drawn with, wrapped about the middle, the twine with which it is tied, and, if the whole bundle is of one colour, there is no need to mention it. Sometimes two colours are employed: 'a garb Or, banded gules'; even three colours is not impossible when the steams and the heads vary. It is then blazoned as stalked (or strawed) of the one colour; eared (or fructed) of another, and banded by a third.

Ears of the various grain plants are common. Sometimes a small bunch is held together, or a number of ears spring from one stem. Rye droops its head, barley is bearded (or aulned), and great delicacy of drawing and sense of design are needed to make them attractive. Many a garb, lacking grace, looks like old Biddy the charwoman with her coarse apron tied too tight.

Pedantic writers make heraldry dismally dull, their ham-fisted illustrators manage to make it not merely unrecognizable, but positively ugly: even the simple, classic, beautiful rose can be rendered like a blot. The heraldic rose is the wild rose, five-petalled and of a softened pentagonal form. In the centre is a circular patch of gold to represent the seeds, and protruding between and beyond the outer circumference of the petals are five green points, representing the calyx out of which the bloom burst. A rose, either argent or gules, is always barbed and seeded proper, or barbed vert and seeded Or, which is the same thing.

The rose, either red or white, survived in sweet simplicity till Tudor times, when the one, of a small diameter, was super-imposed upon the other, as a symbol that the Yorkists and Lancastrians were united. This symbolism is well conceived and

178

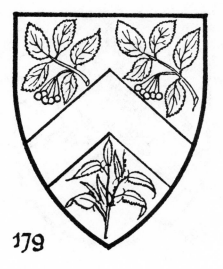

179

the Tudor Rose, as it is called, is itself a thing of beauty, whether the argent debruises the gules, or the gules the argent – a matter determined by the colour of the field – but as the Tudor period advanced, decadence set in. First the rose was slipped, that is, given a short stem and one leaf: next it was slipped and leaved, given a slightly longer stem and two leaves: stalked and leaved followed which resulted in a long stem with numerous leaves. Painting the lily was mere modern improvement compared with ruining the rose. The Tudor Rose was raised to a third layer then it was mutilated and formed into an ungainly compound known as 'a maiden royally crowned proper, crined and vested Or, conjoined to part of a triple rose, red white and red'. Folly could go no further. Today the worst that can happen is that either a simple or a Tudor rose is crowned, and that does not in any way detract from the flower's desirability.

Edward, Earl of Marche, subsequently King Edward IV, had for his badge (cognizance, or cullison), a rose surrounded by rays known as 'rose-in-soleil' – a rose in the sun – and this, too, is not in bad taste.

The sight of exquisite beauty of the wild roses bedecking our peaceful English hedgerows is an aesthetic experience denied to modern youth, for motor roads, concrete posts, and miles of galvanized-iron wire is all this age of martyrdom to the machine can give. Boys and girls think only of the multi-petalled rose of chemical-aided horticulture. This hybrid blossom is on show in modern arms, and is blazoned as 'a cultivated rose', or as 'a garden rose', or even as 'a rose proper', which last term the beginner must be careful not to confuse with a rose barbed and seeded proper.

The rose for the Royal badge of England, for Scotland the thistle. This flower conforms magnificently to an art form since in nature it has long engrailed leaves. The natural plant is purple, but a thistle proper, as it is often blazoned, is vert flowered gules.

For all Ireland the shamrock; the South, though sadly enough severed from us, ought not to abandon it because the North will not. In heraldry it is of course the Royal badge for loyal Northern Ireland only, but as the trefoil it permeates the whole of heraldry. The three foils (or petals) may have shape, and appear each separate, one from the other on their tapering stem, but there is grave danger of that regrettable fellow, the foul draughtsman, turning it into a cross patty fitchy, therefore it is perhaps best to draw it as three circular petals running into each other like an ace of clubs. The trefoil, when acting as the limb terminal of the cross bottonnée or, as it may also be called, trefly, invariably takes the intersecting-circles form.

Given an extra petal the trefoil becomes the quatrefoil which is seldom, if ever, slipped. A fifth petal makes the cinquefoil, whose most important duty is to represent the strawberry flower in which work it assumes the name fraise, and is canting for the surname Fraser, hence often found in Scottish arms.

A further petal makes the sexfoil, never very popular in England, but used much by the French heralds who name it 'angemmes'. To the sexfoil is added two more petals making the octofoil, seldom so called, but, when in use, blazoned as a double quatrefoil.

The cornflower, blazoned as bluebottle, is in appearance like a thistle, and may be 'proper', when it is azure, cupped vert. The gillyflower proper is gules, and the columbine puns perfectly in the achievement of the Worshipful Company of Cooks of the City of London Livery: columbine for *columbina*, Latin for dove, hence, meat for a pigeon pie. The marigold, the sunflower and the heliotrope are drawn the same, even if meant to be different.

The honeysuckle may be blazoned as woodbine, the marguerite as a daisy.

A complete list of the flowers functioning as heraldic charges would be longer than the complete list of the horticulturist, for heraldry includes such strangers as the sengreen, tea, coffee, tobacco and 'flowers gentil'; as well as the 'grain tree', and the 'China cocker tree'.

180

That the fleur-de-lis is an art-form and not a flower, most certainly not a lily-flower, is indicated by the fleur-de-lis and the garden-lily both appearing in the arms of Eton College. The garden-lily is drawn like a tulip, but with the petals curling outward and the stamens visible. Three of them may appear together protruding from the neck of a Grecian vase, the whole composition being blazoned as a lilypot.

The lily-flower does not seem to be employed as an heraldic charge for the sake of its symbolism, but some plants are so used either wholly or in part.

'And laurel for the perfect prime' is a case in point. The wreath seen on the brows of the busts of the Caesars in the Roman Room at the British Museum are not mere sculptor's convention. The laurel wreath was placed on the brow of the triumphant. In heraldry, when a wreath is blazoned but its nature not specified, it is of oak-leaves. The stems, crossed in base, are secured by a bow of ribbon with the ends flotant and the foliage rises in a semicircle at each side to meet at the apex. It may be proper, or of any of the colours, but if simply 'a wreath', without adjectival noun, it remains of oak leaves. Any appropriate foliage may, however, be used: 'a wreath of laurel', 'a wreath of bay'; it may even be of two different plants, 'a wreath of dexter, laurel; sinister, bay'.

A civic wreath, or a garland, is without stems and ribbon, but has clusters of acorns in base, in chief and at each side. A chaplet is a wreath having flowers, if not specified, roses, in place of the garland's acorns. A chaplet graminy is composed of woven grass. Finally, the crest wreath, the wreath of the colours, can appear full circle as a charge. It is a large annulet, compony of twelve pieces alternate metal and tincture, and it carries on its outer circumference four hawks' bells: one in chief, one in base, and one at each side. It may be itself charged, generally with four objects, and then it will be not compony but of either metal or tincture, and is not likely to carry bells. In either form it has a special term, joscelyn or goselyn, hence it is canting in the various branches of the family of Joslin, irrespective of how that surname is spelt.

CHAPTER ELEVEN

Great Guns and Marline Spikes

181

182

THERE is no book, neither is there ever likely to be one, in which is catalogued all the inanimate objects that have made their appearance on the heraldic scene: and there is no man who – notwithstanding a prodigious memory – could retain in mind all of them.

There are, however, a number, in fact a very large number, of such objects that occur again and again, that are common property, to be employed, with discretion, by the learned heralds when devising a coat of arms for an applicant, hence these objects are known as common charges.

Many of them have a symbolic value, others are used for their allusive, or their canting, quality, and yet others to signify a man's calling.

The Worshipful Livery Companies of the City of London are armigerous, and in the majority of their arms will be seen the typical tools of their trades: some have beautiful coats of arms above criticism, the majority have, each, a rather indifferent display, and a few proudly emblazon on their stationery hideous antique home-made jumbles for which the suffering heralds have been unable to refuse confirmation. There are, too, a negligible number still being borne by what is politely called 'prescriptive right'. When a body corporate, or even a private family, has been using unconfirmed arms long enough to be of 'time out of mind' antiquity, it is rather rude to refer to such arms as bogus.

There is a modern book, easily obtainable, dealing with the heraldry of the London Livery Companies,* so the tools of all trades need not be exhibited here: such tools as we mention will be those unlikely to occur in Livery Companies' arms, but on this tour of inspection we will not begin with the workshop: the castle, triple-towered, crenellated, massy, and siegeproof dominates the landscape.

Under the central tower is the port, or doorway, barred either by huge oaken doors or by the portcullis (of which last, more anon). The towers may be provided either with Gothic windows termed lights, or by cruciform archers' niches called loopholes.

The castle is always masoned even though the blazon does not say so and, if the lights and the entrance archway are 'of the field', then peace reigns and doors and windows are open. If they

* John Bromley, *Heraldry of the Guilds of London*, 1960.

are not mentioned, they will be coloured as the castle, and considered closed.

Although this front elevation is normal, a castle may stand arraswise, or 'in perspective'. This does not imply true perspective; it means that the castle is viewed with its corner, not its front, facing the observer.

A square tower is meant to represent a Norman keep, or donjon, and a triangular tower is more or less flat-iron shape, as the famous Castle of Caerlaverock. There are a number of castles drawn in a special way: chief among these one may cite the famous castle on a rock in the arms of the Corporation of the City of Edinburgh.

When the blazon says 'a castle', but does not add 'triple-towered', the edifice intended is a round tower: a tower triple towered has three little round towers issuant of its crenellations.

A portcullis is of course familiar in its general form to everybody: it must be observed, however, that a portcullis in heraldry always appears with a large ring in each of the top corners, and unless the blazon says 'sans chain', from each ring a length of square-linked chain descends. There is a familar, semi-public, Coat of Arms in which may be seen a portcullis sans chains *and rings*, which omissions are not specified in the blazon, but that is merely an error.

In passing, it should be mentioned that all chain in heraldry has square (not oval or round) links.

A castle might stand within a high wall, or bailey, and all cities were so enclosed in the Middle Ages, hence, an essential item of military equipment was the scaling-ladder: a straight section of ladder provided with hooks at the head. When these occur as charges (or as crests) they are likely to be in bend.

If knocking at the castle door or the city gate with the hilt of the sword brought no response (and it did not as a rule!) then some harder knocking was necessary. This was effected by means of the battering-ram which, in heraldry, is said to be armed of its head which is often drawn to represent that of a ram (male sheep). It is also garnished of the two iron bands with suspension rings that surround the body of the instrument.

Artillery ultimately came into the field of battle, and also into the heraldic field. The blazon may say 'guns upon their carriages', when either the old naval, or the corresponding military, gun-carriage must be drawn, but all guns, no matter whether they are called guns, field-pieces, cannon or chambers are of the muzzle-loading type, and, either with or without carriages, they may be blazoned firing, or discharged. The family of Chambers had such an achievement.

The normal projectile from these old guns was a solid iron ball, but there were some fancy shots too, a number of which will be found in coats of arms. The most important of these is the fire-ball, or bomb-shell: a hollow ball filled with inflammable material. It is drawn with its mouth (a round hole simply) in chief and is 'issuant of flames of fire proper' or else it is 'flammant'. Error is often made by ignorant draughtsmen who think to 'improve' a bombshell, by giving it, in chief, a short length of neck for the emission of flames instead of just a round hole. This is a pity, because so drawn it is not merely a decorated bombshell, but is a grenade: a different thing indeed, meant to be thrown by hand, not fired out of big guns. A very good specimen of a grenade may be seen in the badge of the Grenadier Guards.

The earliest 'small-arm' was the matchlock: a musket not fired from the shoulder but supported at the muzzle end in a crutch, and fired by means of a match. Heraldry has its matchlocks, its rests, and its rolls of matches – the last looking like a coil of

183

184

185

186

187

188

string but flammant at the unwound end. Flintlocks, that made their own spark, came later, and pistols, when appearing in arms, are drawn as flintlocks. They may be blazoned as 'petronels'.

The ordinary soldier was probably not at all pleased by the change from bow and arrows to musket. England's archers had been invincible. Sir John Froissart, in his *Chronicles*, cannot refrain from remarking, again and again, on their prowess.

Bows, which may be stringed of another colour, must be orientated – that is to say the blazon must state whether they are to be pale-wise, fess-wise or bend-wise; but arrows, unless otherwise stated, are always pale-wise, and head in base. A sheaf of arrows is the commonest form; one in pale debruised by two in saltire. Arrows are flighted of the feathers and, if the short section of shaft that projects beyond the feathers is to be of a colour differing from that of the shaft, the arrow is described as 'notched'. The arrow head is called the barb, hence the blazon might say, 'a sheaf of arrows, barbed argent, shafted gules, flighted vert and notched azure'.

The bird-bolt is a form of arrow having a short, thick shaft, and it is not barbed: the head is a flattened egg shape. The broad arrow, on the other hand, is never shafted, but is drawn as a shank or socket with a blade extending from each side and inclining backward. When the broad arrow has the rearward edges of the blades engrailed it is a pheon, which is far more common than is the broad arrow.

The beacon, or cresset, in full flame, or fired, or flammant – even inflamed – should be mentioned; so should the caltrap, a spiked device strewn on the plain, to prevent horsemen advancing.

All of the foregoing implements and weapons of war have one point in common: each is either manned by a crew, or is rendered effective by team-work. The individually wielded weapons, skill in the use of which the contestants in the tournaments demonstrated, are the sword, the lance and the battle-axe.

Throughout song and story we meet with swords having magic or mystery; that can be wielded only by an honourable knight, or drawn from the scabbard only by the rightful heir. King Arthur's sword – *Excalibur* – occupies a high place in English legend.

In heraldry the sword, unless blazoned as inverted, is erect and has its point in chief; it is generally proper which is quite correctly argent, but in painting may be given the metallic-blue sheen of tempered steel. Every sword is described as hilted and pommelled (frequently Or) and this includes the cross-piece, or hand-guard (the quillons), the grip, and a ball terminal. It may be hilted of one colour and pommelled of another.

'A sword in its scabbard' has a somewhat coarse appearance, but at the end of the scabbard is depicted a piece of ornamental metal-work, horseshoe-shaped, but with one horn almost twice as long as the other. This, blazoned as the crampette, or the chape, or the boteroll, may stand as a charge in its own right.

A claymore is without quillons, and the grip is not visible since it is inside the 'basket' hand-guard. Daggers and dirks are indistinguishable from swords, and at this point it is well to remind the reader that the weapon in dexter-chief of the arms of the City of London is not, as folk think and books say, the dagger of Sir William Walworth who slew Wat Tyler, but is the Sword of St. Paul, the City's Patron Saint. A broken sword is by no means uncommon – instead of tapering away to its point, it terminates abruptly in a jagged line.

A falchion, a cutlass, a hanger and a sabre are separate names for a weapon that only the experienced swordsman could distinguish between, and which has in heraldry but one form in spite of four names. It is a curved, stout blade, sharp on the convex edge, coming to an obtuse point, rather the shape of an old-time carving knife. When it finishes with a flat end, and the back (concave edge) is engrailed, it is an oriental scimitar. A similar shaped blade with one deep engrailment in the back is the Anglo-Saxon seax. Examples of this may be seen in the bearings of both Essex and Middlesex.

Swords might be brandished by either footmen or cavalry: the lance, however, is a horseman's weapon. The blade, a slender triangle, arises from a shank or socket that joins the shaft: this, which is counter-balanced behind, has a cone-shaped hand-guard. When the point of the lance was lowered, it was helpful to rest the weapon in a steady position. Some breastplates were fitted with a sort of hook for this purpose, but also the shield could be provided with a slot in dexter chief. Shields so drawn are described as à bouche. A broken spear is the 'handle' end: a half-spear the 'business' end.

A battle-axe has the cutting edge facing dexter and the head is in chief. The head may be blazoned as the 'blade', and the shaft as 'the stave'. The Lochaber axe has a crescent shaped blade, hence, a concave cutting edge.

Notwithstanding the warrior's protective armour, these weapons, skilfully handled, could take effect: it was possible to cleave right through the helmet, and to penetrate the breast-plate. In heraldry various pieces of armour are found, but these, like stage-property, belong to no particular period, and are generally badly drawn: few of the close-helmets depicted would be wearable.

The fetterlock could be mistaken for a stirrup were it not that the latter always appears with its strap attached. Saddles, bridles and pack-saddles appear but the most important pieces of horse-ironmongery are the shoe, and the spur.

Horseshoes stand with the horns towards the base, and often terminate in a rather exaggerated scroll representing the 'heel' of the shoe. They should be pierced with seven rectangular nail-holes, four dexter and three sinister. Before Richard I's great seal, all spurs depicted were called pryck-spurs, consisting of a curved spike. On Richard's seal he is seen wearing a rowel spur. A winged spur has the pair of bird-like wings attached to the heel-iron, and in all cases the rowel is in chief.

Another article of great importance that is not unconnected with the horse – or perhaps the sumpter mule – is the water-bouget. The highly conventionalized form it takes conceals its origin and use. In appearance it is like an ornamental capital M, but it represents two water-bags hanging one on each side of a beast of burden, and suspended by straps from a pack-saddle. The conventionalized form is the best. When drawn like a diagram, or a semi-diagram, it is ugly.

Remembering the military origin of heraldry we are not sur-prised at the amount of military equipment, and the appurten-ances of horsemanship that we find among the common charges, but naval affairs and seamanship are not ignored.

Ships of all kinds are to be found, but the heraldic ship, a conventionalized form, called the lymphad is, in many ways, the most suitable.

There was indeed great beauty to be seen in the three-masted clipper-ship who 'ran her eastings down where the strong fair winds of heaven always blow', but when she is to be depicted in arms there is insufficient space to do her justice, and the symbolic lymphad fares much better. She is a galley (and may be so blazoned) with high stern and forecastles, her contour from stem to stern around the keel being semicircular. She is clencher-built, and the lines of her planking should be drawn in: single-masted, has one sail only, and that furled to the yard-arm unless otherwise

189

190

191

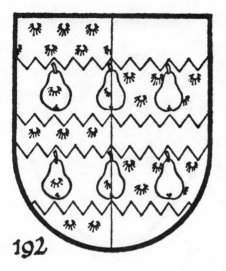

192

193

194

stated. Oars appear over the side, but the rowers are not visible. When the sail is set, it is often itself emblazoned with arms or with badges, and the flotant pennon, always aflutter, need not be plain.

The anchor, symbolic of hope, occurs in arms without maritime significance – it may even be, on occasions, canting. The stock (the crossbar) of the heraldic anchor is called the timber, and it should be drawn to imply that it is of oak and reinforced with wrappings of wire. The anchor ought to appear naked unless blazoned as 'cabled', or as 'chained' when either a length of cordage, or of chain, will descend enwrapping the shank. When this appendage passes the crown of the anchor, it should fall away. If twisted round the flukes it is 'an anchor fouled'.

Though the Army and the Navy are well represented, the Church cannot complain of neglect. Apart from angels and saints, and the insignia of saints, the pall (a Y-shaped vestment), either carrying charges or plain, appears in the arms of several of the episcopal sees, both at home and throughout the Commonwealth. The crozier and the pastoral staff both make many appearances, and not necessarily in ecclesiastical heraldry: for example, see the civic arms of the Corporation of the Municipal Borough of Lambeth where, by its inclusion, the Archbishop's official residence, Lambeth Palace, which is within the Borough bounds, is signalized.

The crozier ought to be a cross patty within an annulet; the pastoral staff, a shepherd's crook; the former carried in solemn procession before an archbishop, the latter before a bishop; but in the Middle Ages 'crozier' was the correct term to describe either shape, hence, in heraldry they often do duty for each other.

The palmer's staff, a walking stick with a ball-shaped handle, and the palmer's scrip (no final 't') or wallet, often appear in the arms of a great traveller, or an explorer. Palmers were pilgrims.

Church bells we have mentioned in passing, when dealing with the furs; here it is necessary to add that the ring by which they are suspended may be blazoned as the cannon, the body of the bell as the barrel, and the rim as the skirt. This is necessary, however, only when these various parts differ from each other in colour. The belfry itself, so blazoned, or as a church tower or spire, occurs occasionally, so does the entire church building. Now and then we come upon a church porch standing alone, and the weathercock from the top of the steeple, blazoned as a vane, is sometimes confused with the vannet, fan, fruttle, scruttle or winnowing basket, all of which are different names for the same thing – an escallop-shell-shaped basket for hand-fanning the chaff from the grain. It is canting in the arms of Robert de Septvans, whose fine brass memorial in Chartham Church, Kent, acts as a magnet to generation after generation of brass-rubbers. His family's motto was: 'The enemies of the King I will disperse like chaff'.*

After the winnowing, the grain went to the mill, which, in its beauty and simplicity, ranks with the clipper-ship among mankind's real achievements. (Mass-produced motor-cars are inferior things.)

The windmill's cruciform sails, often set saltire-wise, appear among crests, but the millstone is met with on the shield. They are drawn slightly in perspective to reveal the stone's thickness, are divided into eight segments by intersecting diameters, and each segment is furrowed parallel with the diameter. English stones were quarried in one piece; continental, imported stones

* See Franklyn, *Brasses*, Arco Publications, 1964.

arrived in eight segments (like a modern round box of cheeses, which has each segment separate, and wedge-shaped).

The stones were held and rotated by means of a heavy forging of sufficient strength to stand the strain. These were flat plates of steel widened by a square section halfway along. This was pierced to correspond to the 'eye' of the stone. Each end of the plate was splayed outward, and this simple piece of smith's craftsmanship makes a most attractive charge. It may be blazoned as a millrind, or as a fer-de-moline, and the central development may be omitted: in fact, when two are set together, cruciform, making the cross moline, the centres must be plain, otherwise it would become a cross moline quadrate. Further the central hole must be omitted or it would be quarterly pierced. Such little traps lie in wait for the unwary copyist, and he is the bane of heraldry.

Mills were manorial property and were not regarded as permanent buildings – in fact, there is a famous print of a mill being drawn on rollers by a huge team of oxen over the downs. Resistance to this sort of rough handling is a recommendation of the builder whose 'art and mistry' is represented in arms by more than mills, castles and churches.

The heraldic arch is delicate, semicircular, keyed at the crown, and supported on columns. The foot of the arch at each side rests on an entablature named, in heraldry, the cap, or capital, or impost; these crown the columns, each of which stands on a base. Differences in colour may distinguish all these parts. A double arch is on three pillars, the central one being shared: a triple arch is on four. Classic columns described by their Greek architectural names may appear without arches.

All common charges do not belong to the big, the brave or the beautiful: very simple domestic appliances have an honoured place, and not least among them is the cauldron, or cooking-pot. When the blazon says 'a pot', but does not specify, it is the cooking-pot that is intended because drinking vessels are college pots, or pewter pots, or possentes: even drinking-horns.

When the meat was served on to the dish, or standish, as it is heraldically called, the pewter pots needed filling with 'jolly good ale, and old'. This heady liquor was drawn from a tun (which may also be blazoned as a barrel, or as a hogshead, or even a tub). The old navy's method of stowing a barrel was 'bung up and bilge free', but heraldry is not quite so particular; as a rule, tuns rest on their bilges (broadest parts) and the bung faces the observer. Some barrels are seen standing on their flat ends, that is, pale-wise, but fess-wise on the bilge is usual.

The coopers, those marvellously skilled craftsmen who made the barrels, also constructed buckets. These, like little half barrels, have two staves upstanding to take a rope handle, and very often three staves downset to act as feet and keep the bucket's bottom free of the ground.

After dinner the ladies might return to their spinning and weaving and embroidering: to represent their work we have many hanks of cotton and silk thread. If the day's work was done they might entertain themselves with music, and instruments are represented in arms. Harps, lyres and violins are prominent stringed instruments. The last is normally in pale, the body chiefward. When the body is to be baseward, it is blazoned as a violin transposed.

Among wind instruments, if precedence is given to that one appearing most frequently, then the bugle-horn has the honour. It is drawn like a cow's horn, the point cut to form a mouth-piece, garnished with two metal bands, and suspended by a cord that finishes in a bow-knot. It is sometimes blazoned as a hunting-horn. Bugle means bull, hence, this instrument is the

195

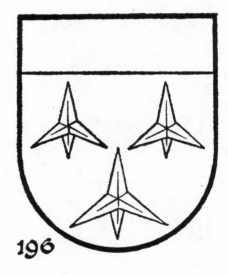

196

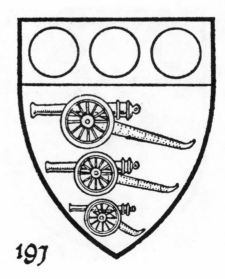

197

198

199

200

true bugle. The short copper trumpet employed for calling orders in an Infantry Regiment is simply a form of trumpet distinguished by the name bugle.

Another wind instrument is drawn as a row of little cylinders, seven in number, each rising higher than the previous one. This is mounted on a frame something like the handle of a hand-saw. It is a perfectly innocent little shepherd's pipe but it is made the victim of much argument. For our purpose, it is a clarion, and we can dispense with the numerous names it has from time to time been given.

Among the amusements of the period was that of playing chess, and though the rules of the game were the same as they now are, a modern player would have been unable to move his pieces, simply because he would not have recognized them. The modern Staunton set, named after its designer, was introduced just about one hundred years ago. Our castle is like a round tower, but before that time the castle, called the rook, was like a cone with the apex cloven and turned outward. Chess rooks make quite attractive charges, but would not be recognizable without pre-knowledge.

This, too, applies, and even more strongly, to the maunch: a sleeve with a long hanging cuff. It may have come into arms in the days when a pair of sleeves was worn as separate from the other garments, and was sometimes dropped by a lady as a token of regard to her chosen knight riding in a tournament. It was for the right to bear 'Or, a maunch gules' that Sir Edward Hastings, rather than relinquish his claim to Lord Grey de Ruthven, spent twenty-six years in prison.* The maunch becomes no problem when, as sometimes happens, it is not an empty sleeve: for example, 'a maunch gules, a hand proper issuant therefrom and holding a crucifix'.

Samples of the hatter's products are not far to seek. In addition to ecclesiastical hats ensigning the shield, various dashing lay hats appear as charges upon it: broad-brimmed hats, felt hats with feathers, tricorne hats, but perhaps the most important (excluding the cap of maintenance) is the humble long-cap (or infula), a fashion started in ancient Rome and never dying. It is the pointed cap, a fool's cap, or brewer's cap or, quite recently when it was again the apex of feminine fashion, the jelly-bag.

The Garter always encircles the shield of a Knight of that most noble Order of chivalry, but it may appear as a charge. It is always buckled, but when buckles thus appear on straps, no special form is given to them. When they appear as charges they may be round or square or oblong, and be called arming buckles or gar-buckles. The tongue should be pendant from the top of the buckle, or from a central bar, but the blazon does not say anything about it. Buckles with tongues pendant are inverted, and the tongue hangs down, outside the frame. There are no jewelled buckles in British heraldry, but we are by no means poverty-stricken. We have our finger-rings which may be 'gemmed' of any given tincture; and the diminutive golden key of the jewel-box, but keys, even when they are of plain iron, are highly decorative charges.

The part of a key that we normally attach to our key-ring is the bow, the part that turns in the lock is called the wards. The normal position for an heraldic key is in pale, bow in base, wards to the dexter. Inverted, the key has its wards, still facing dexter, in base. A key reversed has the bow in base, but the wards facing sinister. It may, too, be inverted and reversed. Back to back (bows in base, wards facing outward) keys are addorsed, and they may be interlaced in the bows – in which

* See Franklyn, *Shield and Crest*.

case it is probable that the bows will not remain plain, but will be ornamented. Bows need not necessarily be oval in shape: some most pleasing effects can be obtained by making square, and other shaped bows.

When fess-wise, keys have their wards towards the chief, bows to the sinister. Keys fess-wise may also be inverted and reversed, but they are likely to have their new position described as 'bows to the dexter'. Keys in saltire normally have wards outward, but they need not: they might even have their bows in chief.

'Argent, three keys sable' will put one erect in each corner, but 'three keys in fess', for example, can be either pale-wise in fess, or fess-wise in fess, and the blazon must say which is intended. The same applies to the other directions.

The ironmonger supplies the shield with more than keys: from him we obtain our various nails, chief among which are Passion nails. If he is in a big way or business he will also supply the five-barred gates we need from time to time – particularly for municipal arms when the town's name ends in 'gate'. He will, perhaps, be able to supply a tent, which he may call a sperver or a pavilion or a tabernacle or a tent-royal. He will not give us tent-pegs or guy-ropes with it. It will just have to balance on its central pennon-bedecked pole.

While in the shop we may ask him if he has a telescope to enable us to study the heraldic heavens. First, even without the glass, we will be aware of 'the sun in his splendour' surrounded by a corona of alternate wavy and straight rays. The sun is either Or or gules unless 'eclipsed' when the disc is sable but the rays remain beaming. Sometimes a demi-sun is issuant in base, or from some other position, even from cloud proper, and such cloud may be distilling drops of rain. This ought to produce the heraldic rainbow, which is Or gules vert and argent.

The moon, when full, is in her plenitude, or in her compliment. She has a halo of fine radiating lines about her. The moon eclipsed may be so blazoned, or else, as in her detriment. Crescent moons have the face in profile on the inner part. When the horns face dexter it ought to be blazoned as 'the moon in her increment', and if facing sinister, as 'the moon in her decrement'. It is, however, quite likely to read 'the moon increscent', or 'the moon decrescent'.

Stars have six wavy points, and are called estoiles. All the signs of the Zodiac and the Planetary (also called the alchemical) symbols appear with comets, or blazing stars (bearded of the tail) and with thunderbolts. Sometimes called Jupiter's thunderbolt, it is a long, slender barrel, winged, emitting smoke and fire at each end, and having behind it a saltire of forked lightning. One is to be seen in the fore paw of a lion, acting as crest for the British Broadcasting Corporation.

The astrologer, and the astronomer, the alchemist and the magician, were often one and the same person. They distilled weird essences out of alembics (or retorts) and sought, by magic, to transmute the metals. To this end they inscribed magical signs, including the Double Delta, or Shield of David, or Solomon's Seal, which consists of two equilateral triangles interlaced; or perhaps they gave preference to the pentagram, a five-pointed figure constructed in one continuous line. Both of these, as well as the planetary and Zodiacal signs, survive in modern heraldry.

If these doughty experimenters gassed themselves, poisoned themselves, or blew themselves up, the surgeon was sent for and he applied the only remedy he knew: he let blood. To this end he employed a knife, something like an open razor, but

201

202

203

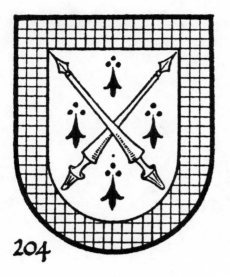

204

with an extension on the sheath, making a kind of S-shaped handle: this, called a phleam (or fleme, or phlegm) frequently distinguishes the arms of a great doctor, or of a medical institution. In the same way the fasces, the lictors, the bundle of rods round the haft of an axe, the Roman symbol of authority, will appear in arms of both lawyers and civic dignitaries.

CHAPTER TWELVE

Revelations of Arms

A COAT OF ARMS is, in lawyer's language, an incorporeal hereditament: During the hearing of the action in the 1954 Court of Chivalry, the Surrogate, Lord Chief Justice Goddard, was in favour of this view, but Cole, A. C., Portcullis Pursuivant, Council for the Defendant, cast doubt upon it. In other words, although it is not of a material nature, it passes from father to son, but unlike a house, or money, or any other form of realty which automatically goes to the eldest son, or, failing him, to the next of kin, and normally becomes the inheritor's sole property for the time being, the possession of arms is equally the birthright of all offspring, both male and female. The armorial insignia is the inalienable property of a family and of each individual member of it: but in Scotland it must, and in England it ought to, reveal who, within the family, is who.

When family arms have been in use for centuries, the head of the house, his children and grandchildren, his nephews and nieces, his cousins and his second and third cousins, and others 'removed' to a great distance of relationship, being descendants of an armigerous common ancestor, all bear the same arms notwithstanding that they do not necessarily know each other.

Since the first function of the heraldic device is to enable the bearer to be recognized, this undeniable multiple ownership seems to strike at the very root of the system. It was a practical difficulty recognized in the earliest days of the science when a man and his eldest son could both be engaged in the same military operation, and it was promptly and effectively solved: on the son's shield, a little below the chief, and debruising all charges that might already be occupying the position, was painted a narrow, fess-wise stripe, and depending from it, three similarly narrow projections.

When this had been done the arms were described as differenced with a label of three points. At first it was sufficient for only the eldest son to difference because, arms being in practical daily employment, his younger brothers who were not leading a contingent in time of war, nor being active and authoritative in manorial and in national administration in times of peace, could not be confused with him.

Later, when the hard contours of the feudal system softened, armorial bearings became more personal and less military and administrative in their use, and differences were devised for cadets.

205

206

207

208

209

These marks of difference, or of cadency, or brisures, as they may be variously named, are theoretically still in use. The modern label does not extend right across the shield. It does not exceed half of the shield's width, and may be rather less than that: further, it is not of a metal. The label throughout (full width of the shield) argent, is reserved, in England, to members of the Royal Family. In Scotland, labels throughout are customary for commoners.

The brisure of the second son is a crescent; of the third, a mullet; of the fourth, a martlet; of the fifth, an annulet; of the sixth, a fleur-de-lis; of the seventh, a rose; of the eighth, a cross moline; and of the ninth, a double quatrefoil.

Brisures, not being charges, do not conform to the colour rule: tincture may rest upon tincture; and, to aid the eye, brisures should be smaller, in proportion, than they would be were they charges. For example, 'azure, three mullets argent; a mullet for difference'. If the brisure was the same size as the charges it would appear as four mullets, three in chief and one in base. Centre chief is the normal position for a brisure, but if that is ungainly, ugly or inconvenient – if, for example, there is a charge in centre chief – the brisure may go elsewhere. Its size and colour will distinguish it. On the ordinary, when there is one, is a good place.

Thus far, differencing seems simple, and if it actually were, perhaps the brisures would be regularly used instead of being universally ignored as they are in English arms. (Scotland has its own system – very different from England's – and there, no man except 'chief of a name' wears undifferenced arms.)

The first anomaly in English differencing is the fact that the second son of the first son is differenced the same as his uncle who is second son of the grandfather. To prevent this, the mark of difference is supposed to become a 'house' mark, and the brisure of the individual to be placed on it, thus all the sons of a second son are members of the second house, each of them should difference with a crescent for his 'house', and on the crescent the second son of this house will deposit another crescent: if three generations were all using arms we might expect a crescent on a crescent on a crescent which is absurd anyway, and because the first crescent is smaller than a charge it is impossible – the third would be microscopic.

It will be observed that we have not used for our examples a first son of a first son. The reason is that although the label is the difference employed by the first son it is so used only because he is the heir-apparent. His son – the eldest grandson – is the heir-presumptive, and wears a label of five points. Were the eldest son to meet an untimely end, a situation, alas, all too common in wartime, the heir-presumptive becomes the heir-apparent, abandons his label of five points, and assumes one of three points, although he is not the eldest son of the head of the family.

It may also have been noted that no reference has been made to marks of difference used by the daughters of the family: again, there is a very good reason. Females do not qualify for cadency. A woman cannot be an heir-apparent, and all sisters, notwithstanding disparity in ages, inherit, on the death of the father (when there is no brother), equal portions in a family property. Under these circumstances ladies need no marks of difference. This should not be considered another example of injustice to women but rather as a privilege in which the brothers share only by default: slightly more attention was given to differencing when coach panels were emblazoned, but now it is only shopkeepers and corporations who paint arms on motor-vehicles and one needs no indicator of the age of a dust-cart.

It is not only to declare the cadency of brothers that marks of difference appear in a coat of arms. The need arises from other causes, and although such marks cannot be called either marks of cadency, or brisures, they are still for difference or, more correctly, distinction.

Among these marks, and introduced as recently as 1950, is the mascle. This serves to difference the arms of a divorced woman who, after the dissolution of her marriage, must, if she desires to display arms, revert to her paternal bearings on a lozenge: hence, without the mark of distinction, she and her spinster sister were armorially indistinguishable one from the other. (In Scotland the arms of the guilty party are debruised of an abatement.)

Special social conditions attract marks of distinction; an adopted son, for instance, may receive a confirmation of his right to use his foster-father's arms 'suitably differenced', and although fashions in these specialized differences rule for a time, there is no universally accepted mark for any particular category. We know, of course, that there is no such thing as a 'bar sinister', and that the term is a vulgar euphemism, but it remains to be said that a bend sinister, or a baton sinister (as if it could be dexter!) or even a baston, are not always marks of difference to indicate the wearer's status. Such elements of armorial composition may, from time to time, have been employed as differences indicating that the person whose arms are so marked is not in the line of inheritance, but they do not invariably serve that end, and must not be so interpreted on sight.

Cadency marks can become permanent residents in an achievement, and appear in the arms of each member of that branch of a family, including females. This happens when two well-established families are descended from a common ancestor. The Blanckes of Surrey have held land in that county for more than six hundred years, and not one of them has ever met a member of the Blenke family of Northumberland, but both families bear the same arms, and to distinguish between them, the Blanckes of Surrey have, and have had time out of mind, a brisure for difference: both families trace their descent from Roger de Blanke who held a manor in Dorset, and whose grandfather is assumed to have been Roque de Blenque who was among the Companions of William Duke of Normandy, and whose name and arms appear in the Roll of Battle Abbey – at least, in one of the six spurious versions of that totally spurious document.

A man's own endeavours may secure for him a mark of distinction among which is the standardized and easily recognizable badge of the baronet. This is added to the arms when the elevation is gazetted, and it remains in position in perpetuity because the rank of a baronet is hereditary. 'On an escutcheon argent a sinister hand erect, apaumée, couped at the wrist, gules.' It generally occupies, as a brisure does, the centre chief, but it may go elsewhere, and further, it may alter its form slightly: the hand may appear on a canton.

Another addition to arms that a man may win, and that becomes hereditary but is not standardized, is the augmentation of honour which his heirs and descendants for ever may bear with justifiable pride.

Augmentations can be conferred only by the Sovereign, and they betoken Royal gratitude for services rendered. Such services may be of either a personal, or of a State character. King Charles II bestowed augmentations of honour on his friends who served and sustained him: Nelson received augmentations for his victories.

There have been occasions when a devoted subject, hitherto non-armigerous, has been granted arms by Royal Warrant.

210

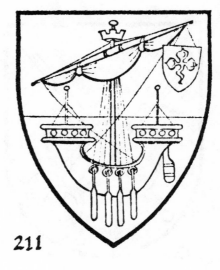

211

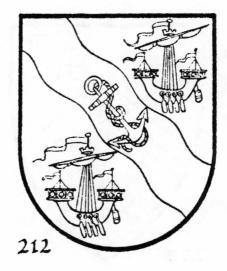

212

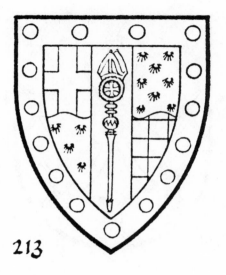

213

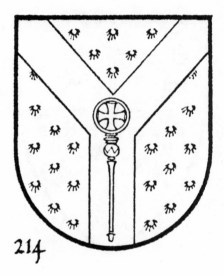

214

215

Such achievements are Arms of Augmentation. An outstanding example of loyalty and devotion is that of Colonel Carlos,* whose warrant bears the signature of King Charles II. No one, not even the Lord Lyon King of Arms has the power to make an alteration to such arms.

Very often the addition to an existing achievement consists of a crest, or of an extra crest. This may be done in addition to augmenting the shield.

Early augmentations were simple, and though they may have the effect of rather overcrowding the shield they do not destroy its beauty. Later the habit of employing the chief and the canton in augmentation grew. This has first, the ill-effect of depressing the original contents of the shield into a squat, often ungainly, shape, which is bad enough, but the object of the augmentation is generally to be allusive hence these appalling chiefs were besmeared with entire battle scenes and major naval engagements. Nelson's originally simple arms were almost obliterated by these 'blushing honours thick upon him!'

In blazon the shield is fully described in the normal way then follows 'and, in augmentation of honour, upon a chief . . .'. Often, far too often, this formula is reversed 'and as an honourable augmentation, upon a chief . . .'. Since an augmentation is an addition, a dishonourable augmentation would be an abatement (or rebatement) of honour. It is doubtful whether such things ever did exist – they may have done because there is never smoke without fire – but it is certain that if they did they were invariably of the colour named tenné, a chestnut brown, still avoided in British arms, and known as the stainand colour.† It must, however, be emphasized that when the words 'honourable augmentation' occur they refer to augmentation of honour and do not imply rebatement.

There are examples of achievements quartered in augmentation, and of others quartered for difference, but the primary purpose of quartering is to express union.

At this juncture it seems wise to point out that a coat of arms quarterly is not necessarily for difference, for augmentation or for union: often it is only the field quarterly, and is merely a variation, but even if each canton is charged with a different device, it may be a simple first grant.

The grouping together of more than one achievement for display within the confines of one shield is called marshaling. Many people, among them those who ought to know better, entertain the idea that multiplicity of quarters is indicative of high aristocratic origin, hence, there is a tendency for armigers to pile up (in good faith and utter folly), quarters to which they have no title whatsoever. Some of this stupid home-made marshaling would be legitimate in Continental countries, but here it is as bad as the bearing of totally bogus arms. There is no limit placed upon the number of quarters in an English achievement: the control is exerted only in the fulfilment of conditions. In Scotland the number displayed is restricted to four, but a man may be acknowledged to legitimately possess a greater number.

Marshaling, expressive of union, is, in modern times, used mainly to reveal marital union, but in the feudal age it frequently

* See *Shield and Crest*.

† Recently an applicant for a grant of Arms received stainand colours, it having been decided that several centuries of tradition could be cancelled by an official violation. The Armiger thus fooled is constantly enquiring why people who understand heraldry begin to laugh when they see the achievement of which he is so proud, but even his best friends will not tell him.

indicated union of estate for reasons other than marriage, and
even today it is not always eloquent of marriage.

The earliest method of indicating the union of families was
for the husband (in heraldry referred to as the baron), to add to
his own arms one charge from the achievement of his wife's
family. These mixtures were known as arms composed. The
system was a bad one, being causative of confusion, and there
grew up the custom of cutting the arms of man and wife (baron
et femmé) in half along the palar line, and assembling them
together, the dexter half of the husband's with the sinister half
of the wife's. This method, named dimidiation, proved worse
than arms composed. It sometimes happened that the halving
made each achievement unrecognizable, and the assembling
produced a freak. This was very likely to happen when both
fields were of the same colour. Some of these queer mixtures are
still with us: in public arms we see the dexter half of a lion
passant, or of a fish naiant, dimidiating the sinister half of the
hulk of a ship. In blazon one always describes the dexter side
first, thus: 'Argent, a bend gules, dimidiating (or dimidiated
with) gules a chevron argent.' The result of this is utter deception to the eye of the beholder who sees, 'per pale argent and
gules, a bend counterchanged', which happens to be the arms of
Geoffrey Chaucer.

Out of dimidiation grew impalement, the system that is still
in use. The baron et femmé achievement thus marshaled has
the whole of the husband's arms on the dexter, and the whole of
the wife's arms on the sinister. Each half is blazoned separately:
'gules, a fess between three bugle-horns argent garnished vert,
impaling ermine, on a saltire azure between four fleur-de-lis gules,
a mullet Or.' The names of the contracting parties might be
given: 'argent three ogresses, for *Jimpson*; impaling Or, three
crosses-crosslet azure for *Gildersbrough*.' If either of the impaled
achievements had been within a bordure, it would be omitted
along the palar line.

The offspring of this marriage do not display their parents'
dual impaled achievement which expresses the union of the two
families represented, and which may be used by either the man
or his wife. Their sons and daughters display the paternal arms
only, because family inheritance is patrilineal – their name is
Jimpson, not Gildersbrough. Their cousins, named Gildersbrough, being offspring of the mother's brother, use the arms of
Gildersbrough and have no blood connection whatsoever with
Jimpson.

Impalement that is not expressive of matrimonial alliance
takes place when a man is appointed to an office that is itself
ennobled by arms. An Episcopal See is thus dignified: the
Archbishop or the Bishop, for the duration of his term of office,
displays dexter, the arms of the See, impaling sinister his own
family arms. There is no personal preference: a Bishop does not
himself decide upon his armorial display, he simply conforms to
custom and follows the tradition that his predecessors in offices
have followed. The Archbishop of Canterbury does likewise,
hence, the following paragraph which appeared in the *Daily Tele-
graph* on 27 June, 1961, is inexplicable:

'The Archbishop of Canterbury ... has had his own full-
sized flag made – an innovation for the Primate of all England.
It bears his personal arms – a mitre and shield – on a blue
background, and is flown on his instructions to show that he is
in residence.'

Apart from usurpation of authority, this display is of ignorance rather than of arms. A personal banner would, even if
conforming to the rules for a personal banner, be the wrong
thing for an Archbishop to fly officially, but the description is

216

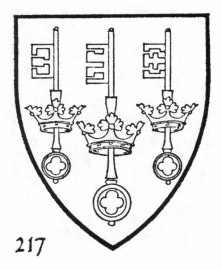

217

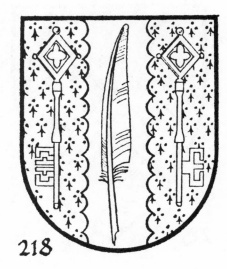

218

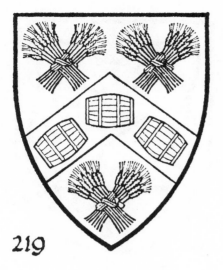

219

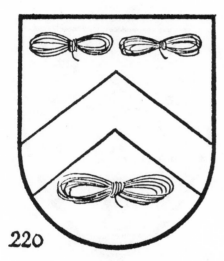

220

220A

that of an outsized trumpet-banner, to which the Primate of all England is not entitled.

In Scotland the Lord Lyon King of Arms has both the authority and the power to prevent such an occurrence. In England the Kings of Arms have authority but not power. Garter King of Arms* could do no more than write a polite letter of protest in which he might call the attention of the offender to his own impaled achievement printed in his letter heading, for Kings of Arms have arms of office; so do the Regius Professors of Cambridge University.

If the holder of an armigerous office is married, he cannot marshal the three achievements on one shield, not because marshaling by three is prohibited, but because he does not share the office with his wife, hence, his total display has to reveal two unrelated alliances.

To effect this, two shields are employed, and they appear side by side, or accolée: on the dexter a shield in which the man's arms are impaled with those of his office; on the sinister, his arms impaling those of his wife. In these circumstances, not only are offspring of the marriage unable to display the assembly, but the wife cannot do so, and upon retirement the man himself cannot – the Arms of Office go to his successor.

An ordinary marital impalement will, naturally, cease to exist if the marriage is dissolved, but there are, too, circumstances under which impalement is abandoned, although the marriage endures and propinquity is maintained. The conditions that break impalement open the way to quartering.

Notwithstanding that a woman cannot be heir-apparent, she can become heir if her father dies without male issue (or without surviving male issue).

An heraldic heiress is one who thus inherits family arms even though there may be nothing else for her to inherit. A number of sisters become heiresses but this circumstance does not involve any complications: what applies to an only daughter will apply to each of a number of sisters.

On her marriage, her paternal arms are impaled with those of her husband, but following the death of her father simple impalement is no longer correct. The husband's arms return to the full width of the shield, and the wife's are displayed on an inescutcheon which, when that of an heraldic heiress, is an escutcheon of pretence because her husband is pretender to her family honour, there being no other living male who will maintain it.

Only the husband and wife can display the joint arms in this form, but the offspring of this marriage are in a different position from the sons and daughters of a woman who has a brother. They inherit, through the father, the arms of the mother to which he was himself pretender hence, they become possessed of two coats of arms.

The inescutcheon being the indicator of marriage to, not descent from, an heiress, cannot go to the next generation, hence, to display the arms of both families they quarter. The shield, party per pale and per fess, is emblazoned in dexter chief and in sinister base with the arms of the father, and in sinister chief and dexter base, those of the mother. The entire composition is blazoned by numbers; the description of each quarter or pair of quarters being completed before the next in numerical order which, however many quarters there may be, runs from dexter to sinister and from chief to base.

In a simple quarterly-of-four achievement uniting only two

* Garter King of Arms is also Her Majesty's Inspector General of flags.

families, each appears twice and the quarters are grouped together: 'first and fourth (or, one and four) argent, a fess sable, for *Aye*: second and third (or two and three), sable, a pale argent for *Bee*.' Another method of expressing so simple a marshaling is, 'argent, a fess sable for *Aye*: quarterly with sable, a pale argent, for *Bee*.' If the arms are very famous, even less will say as much: 'France Ancient quarterly with England.'

The dexter chief contains the pronominal coat of arms, and in a big system of quarters where the total would be an odd number, a final quarter is added and in it the pronominal coat is repeated; 'quarterly of twenty: one and twenty, Or, a chevron gules, for *Down*, two . . .' and so on, to nineteen.

In writing such a blazon of marshaling, the numbers of the quarters ought always to appear in Roman figures: this, as will appear later, is the only way in which to prevent confusion, and the fact of Arabic numerals being used in many books is not to the credit of the authors.

It ought, perhaps, to be specifically pointed out that quarters accumulate only through marriages to successive heiresses, not merely by marriage to a woman who is the daughter of an armiger, and who has a brother or brothers.

Starting with I and IV for the father, and II and III for the mother, marriage with another heiress will not increase the number of quarters; it will merely alter the appearance which will become I and IV, pronominal; II, the new heiress; III, the first heiress. A further marriage with an heiress will replace the repetition in IV, and after that the number of quarters will increase. This may not necessarily be confined to the addition of one only at a time. If a marriage is contracted with an heiress who is herself descended from a father with numerous quarters, she brings in all of them: thus the young man with twenty quarters who marries the heiress with forty, transmits to his own son sixty quarters, all of the father's parading in numerical order before all of the mother's.

Sixty quarters are too many to be of practical service because each would be so small that, in all normal uses, to be distinguished a lens would be necessary, hence, when marshaling has gone thus far it is customary to use the pronominal coat of arms only. There may, however, be among the quarters the arms of some very distinguished men with whom one wishes to claim connection. To do so, one must display the chain of achievements by which the arms are brought in: to simply quarter the pronominal arms with that of the person one wishes to claim would imply that he was one's own grandfather, when in fact he has been brought in on the distaff side through, probably, more than one female.

Normally these marital relationships are expressed in quarters by the Officers of Arms acting within their own right: there are, however, some coats of arms quartered by Royal Licence. This is done in respect of a 'name and arms clause' in a will which lays down that a daughter shall inherit subject to her husband using her family name and arms. The result is a hyphenated name, and a quarterly-of-four coat of arms that is in effect a new grant and is indivisible. When absorbed in a greater number of quarters it becomes a grand quarter, that is, a quarter which is itself divided into sub-quarters. These, in written blazon, are numbered in Arabic figures, and are verbally referred to as subquarters. In Scotland, where four quarters is the limit, in one shield, each may be a grand quarter, thus giving the visual impression of sixteen.

The general rules of marshaling are flexible, as indeed they must be, since circumstances alter cases, and many complications

220B

221

222

223

224

225

have to be considered and catered for, but the basic idea does not change, and it is seldom that a completely new rule has to be introduced.

A certain complication exists when a peer has an only daughter. On the death of her father she will become a peeress in her own right, and her lozenge of arms will be displayed between the peerage supporters. If her husband is a commoner, he cannot place his shield, bearing her escutcheon of pretence, between supporters hence, the inescutcheon, ensigned with her coronet of rank, is displayed on her husband's shield, and accolée is a lozenge of her arms between its supporters. This accolée arrangement would be necessary if her husband were himself a peer, for each has separate supporters.

The next generation quarters in the ordinary way. The peeress' son inherits his mother's title and supporters, and (when his father is a commoner) indicates, by his pronominal quarter, that the peerage has been transferred from one family to another. The son of a marriage between a peeress in her own right and a peer, is in the same position, but he inherits four supporters – those of both his father and his mother. The quartered shield will appear between his father's dexter and his mother's sinister supporter, but when the two titles take effect separately, as for example between Scotland and England, the two separate achievements may be used.

It will be seen that a coat of arms, kept up to date, reveals not only family history, but the life story of the armiger. In order that it may speak the truth, it is well for the changes to be made by the Officers of Arms. Even so simple and obvious a marshaling as an impalement ought not to be taken for granted. Armigers who think they know what they are entitled to, do well to make sure, and the Lyon office in Scotland and the College of Arms in England are the places where certainty dwells.

It is essential to avoid – like the plague that they are – 'Practitioners' and 'Armorists', and other parasites who batten on public ignorance. They are easy to find, for they advertise blatantly. Many a man who believes he bears arms in right of his ancestors is deeply shocked and hurt if he finds at length that one of his forbears fell a victim to such a charlatan. They used to be called 'Heraldic Stationers'; today, however, stationers who supply heraldically embellished notepaper are simple tradesmen who do not set themselves up as either 'Armorists' or 'Practitioners'. They do not, as a rule, claim to be genealogists, but they will 'take orders', and may, quite innocently, pass the inquiry on to a person who will, for a fee, find any ancestors the customer would like – Blood Royal costs extra.

The reorganization of London's Local Government is providing a happy hunting ground for huxters of Arms. We read in the daily press that one Authority is 'consulting a well-known firm of designers of Arms,' that another is setting a 'competition' for its citizens to enter.

Town clerks should be aware that arms produced by well-known firms, or by the local school-children will, if used, be spurious. The Kings of Arms, and they alone, have the mandate to grant Arms.

Down to the end of the nineteenth century the armorial mourning board, called a hatchment, was displayed over the doorway of a house of mourning. It was about six feet square, was set up lozenge-wise, and on it was painted the arms of the deceased with a black background. It told the observer whether a bachelor, a spinster, a husband, a wife, a widower or a widow had died.

Arms on a shield, without impalement, and with a full black background were those of a bachelor; an impaled shield with a

black background to the dexter-side only indicated that a widow
was left; an impaled shield with a full black background showed
that the wife was already dead.

An unimpaled lozenge was that of a spinster; an impaled
lozenge, that of a widow. When the hatchment had to convey
the information that a man had lost his wife the black background appeared only on the sinister half. After the funeral the
hatchment was hung in the local church for a minimum period
of a year and a day. Finally, on the funerary monument, be it of
stone or of brass, there appears the armorial bearings of the
deceased; thus is he identified to posterity.

228

226

227

229

230

Blazon of Illustration

FIGURES preceding each item refer to the number of the illustration.

1. Argent, a cross of St. George; on a chief azure a ducal coronet within the garter between, dexter, a lion passant gardant and, sinister, a fleur-de-lis, all Or, *impaling* Sable, a lion Or holding between the forepaws the dexter half of a wheel: the whole ensigned with a King of Arms crown gold, the cap gules tasselled Or. *Sir Anthony Richard Wagner, K.C.V.O., D.Litt., F.S.A., Garter Principal King of Arms*

2. Argent, a lion sejant affrontée with forepaws extended gules, armed and langued azure, holding in the dexter paw a thistle proper, and in the sinister an escutcheon of the second: on a chief azure the cross of St. Andrew, *impaling* Quarterly I and IV argent, three mullets azure, a bordure chequy of the first and second charged with three crescents gules (for Innes): II Gules, three boars' heads erazed Or, armed proper, langued sable (for Aberchirder of that Ilk and Kinnairdy); III, Or, a fess ermine between three griffins' heads erazed vert, langued gules (for Breber of Learney), the whole ensigned with a King of Arms Crown gold, the cap gules tasselled Or, and in front of two Batons of Office in saltire proper. *Sir Thomas Innes of Learney, K.C.V.O., LL.D., F.S.A. (Scots.), Lord Lyon King of Arms*

3. Ermine, two barrulets wavy Or between as many bats displayed sable, within a bordure azure. *Lord Heyworth*

4. Argent, crusily-fitchy sable, a chevron ermines between three mill-rinds of the second pierced of the field: a chief of the third. *Kingsmill*

5. Per bend sinister ermine and ermines, a lion rampant Or, on a chief azure three crosses moline of the third. *Young*

6. Vair, a lion rampant Or between two roses in fess argent and, in base, an annulet of the second. *Jones*

7. Tierced in pairlee; I, vert, a torteau charged with a cross patonce Or within an annulet Ermine: II, Purpure, III, Azure: in each, a rose argent barbed and seeded proper and issuant therefrom a sprig of oak leaved vert, acorned Or, and overall a basket-hilted broadsword [claymore] pale-wise, proper, along the palar line. A spurious composition

8. Gyronny, Or and azure, on a chief argent a fleur-de-lis between two crescents gules. *Prentice*

9. Gules, two bars between three mullets argent. *Scarysbrooke*

10. Per fess Or and sable, a bend charged with three annulets, all counterchanged. *Abraham*

11. Argent, on a pale engrailed sable, three crescents Or. *Asheley*

12. Argent, on a bend engrailed between two cotisses sable, three mullets of the field. *Andrews*

13. Per pale Or and sable a chevron counterchanged. *Flegg*

14. Gyronny of eight ermine and gules, charged on each piece with a mullet Or. *Campbell*

15. Argent, a chevron sable between, in chief, two sheaves of arrows gules banded of the first; and in base, a bugle-horn of the second stringed and garnished Or. *Duncanson*

16. Or, on a chevron between three annulets gules, as many crescents argent. *Charterhouse*. (With the crescents of the field, for *Sutton*, Bishop of Lincoln, 1280–1299, the founder.)

17. Gules, on a plain bend between two cotisses indented Or, three mullets of the first. *Marmabell*

18. Or, two bendlets gules, and in chief three torteaux. *Blumworth*

19. Sable, two bendlets raguly between as many hawks argent: on a chief of the last, on a pale azure between two fleurs-de-lis of the field, a cross patonce of the second. *Bradshaw*

20. Gules, three bendlets dancetty Or. *Mondatt*

21. Argent, a fess embattled, in chief two mullets sable. *Twining*

22. Argent, a fess embattled-counter-embattled cottised plain between three annulets gules. *Viall*

23. Or, a palm-tree eradicated proper between, on the dexter, a pomegranate also proper, and on the sinister a branch of laurel fructed vert: on a chief azure, a lion passant of the first, in the dexter paw a rod erect, gold. *Sassoon*

24. Or, a fess dancetty; and for distinction, in dexter chief a cross-crosslet fitchy. *Vavasour* (first and fourth quarter of Vavasour of Hazlewood)

25. Or, three pallets gules each charged with an escallop of the first. *Earle*

26. Per pale, vert and azure, four mascles interlaced in fess Or between as many crosses-crosslet in saltire argent. *Thornycroft*

27. Argent, six chevronelles alternately gules and sable. *Farleigh*

28. Or, on a bend indented gules, three estoiles of the first. *Lord Michelham*

29. Per fess sable and gules, a fess indented between two mascles in chief, and bugle-horn stringed in base, all Or. *Mitchell*

30. Per fess nebuly sable and argent, a pale with three hinds' heads erazed, two and one; and as many annulets one and two all countercharged. *Bowlby*

31. Azure, on a cross engrailed argent a civic wreath vert, and in the quarter* a trefoil slipped Or. *Brooks*

32. Argent, a cross of St. George, and in dexter chief* a sword erect gules. *Corporation of the City of London*

33. Argent, a saltire engrailed gules, a chief also engrailed azure, the latter charged with a fraise of the first. *Tweedie*

34. Per pale argent and Or, a saltire parted and fretty gules, on a chief of the last a billet within an annulet between two fleurs-de-lis of the second. *Taylor*

35. Azure, a naval crown between four crosses-crosslet all within a cross resarcelly disjointed between as many crosses-crosslet, all Or. *Knowles*

36. Sable, a cross parted and fretty between, in dexter chief, an anchor erect and, in sinister base, a cinquefoil Or. *Moresby*

37. Argent, on a cross flory gules between four pommes, a mullet between as many crescents Or. *Toler*

38. Quarterly, per pale indented ermine and gules guttée d'or, a fess nebuly of the last between first and fourth a lion's head couped azure; second, a pair of wings conjoined in leure of the third, and in dexter base quarter a chess-rook argent. *Cawthorne*

39. Azure, on a pile invected argent between two roses in base of the second, barbed and seeded proper, a lion passant of the field. *Barnato*

40. Chequy azure and argent, on a pile Or, two roses gules, barbed and seeded proper, and a fleur-de-lis of the fourth. *Parkinson*

41. Or, three piles gules each charged with a bugle-horn stringed of the first: a chief vair. *Basset*

42. Sable, three piles conjoined in point argent; on a chief gules, a lion passant Or. *Hacket*

43. Or, a lion rampant regardant sable, on a canton azure, a cross paty-fitchy of the first. *Lloyd* (of Lossett)

44. Argent, a fleur-de-lis sable; in dexter chief a mullet vert. *Gayre.* (Lt.-Col. Gayre of Gayre and Nigg, the Much Honoured the Laird of Gayre)

45. Gules, on a fess engrailed between five billets, three and two, Or, three roses of the field barbed and seeded proper. *Beauchamp* (of New Zealand)

46. Per pale azure and Or, three lozenges conjoined in fess counterchanged; on a chief enarched argent two foxes' heads erazed of the first. *Freeman*

47. Vert, a cross of seven lozenges conjoined, three in fess and five in pale, ermine; between two flaunches ermines. *Whittingstall*

48. Gules, five fusils conjoined in bend Or between two Norman pillars of the last each charged with a cross-crosslet fitchy of the field. *Eykyn*

49. Argent masoned sable, two crescents in pale of the second between as many flaunches azure each charged with a cross fleury Or. *Mason* (of Gawthorp)

50. Ermine, a crescent gules, on a chief indented azure three ducal coronets Or. *Litton*

51. Per fess wavy azure and argent; in chief, an increscent between two estoiles Or and, in base, three barrulets wavy of the first. *Lund*

52. Sable, three ears of wheat slipped and leaved erect argent, banded Or, between, in fess, a descrescent and an increscent of the second, all within a bordure of the same charged with seven estoiles each of five rays gules. *Moon*

53. Ermine, a chevron azure charged with another Or, thereon three heurtes: on a chief sable as many crosses-crosslet of the third. *Paul*

54. Azure, on a chevron Or between three bezants as many laurel-leaves slipped vert, all within a bordure wavy argent. *Hope*

55. Per fess gules and ermine fretty sable, in chief two plates. *Platt*

56. Sable, three plates; on a chief argent a unicorn's head erazed of the first between two pellets. *Punchard*

57. Argent, a bend engrailed azure between, in chief, a bull's head erazed of the last gorged with an antique crown Or and, in base, a fountain. *Ratcliffe*

58. Sable, a bend engrailed ermine, on a chief argent an escallop gules between two torteaux. *Browne*

59. Sable guttée d'eau; in chief, two antique lamps fired proper and, in base, the sun in his splendour Or. *Willey*

60. Argent, guttée d'poix; a lion rampant azure between two flaunches of the last each charged with a bear's gambe erazed and erect, argent. *Pickering*

61. Azure, semé-de-lis Or, a lion rampant argent. *Poole*

62. Vert guttée d'or, two bendlets sinister raguly, between as many mullets of six points Or pierced of the field. *Ovey*

63. Per chevron, in chief lozengy argent and sable, in base vert a lion sejant gardant Or. *Old*

64. Per chevron argent and gules billety counterchanged. *Beliald*

65. Barry-nebuly of six argent and vert; in dexter chief a falcon close belled Or. *Falkner*

66. Or, a fess chequy azure and argent between, in chief, two crescents gules and, in base, a boar's head couped close sable, all within a bordure invected of the second and charged with three crosses-crosslet fitchy of the first. *Clerk*

67. Argent, between two estoiles in fess argent, a figure representing Justice vested of the last, in the dexter hand a sword erect proper, in the sinister, a pair of scales Or. *Wergman* (Surrey)

68. Gules, a man in armour shooting from a crossbow proper, an arrow to the sinister. *O'Loghlen*

69. Azure, three woodmen in fess proper each bearing on his dexter arm an escutcheon argent charged with a cross gules, and on his sinister shoulder his club of the second: on a canton ermine three lozenges conjoined in fess sable. *Viscount Halifax of Mount Bretton* (family name. *Wood*)

* Nos. 31 and 32: observe the two different modes of expression – '. . in the quarter . . .' and '. . . in dexter chief'. The former is archaic.

70. Per fess sable and Or, a pale counterchanged, three boys' heads afrontée couped at the shoulders two and one proper, and as many serpents knowed one and two vert. *Price* (of *Glynllech*)

71. Per saltire argent and gules a cross potent counter-changed within a bordure indented sable charged with four human hearts and as many fleurs-de-lis alternate Or. *Skeet*

72. Sable, a thigh-bone in pale, surmounted by another in fess argent between two crosses paty in bend, Or. *Baines*

73. Gules, a lion rampant argent, a bordure compony of the last and sable, bezanty. *Gray* (of *Gray's Inn*)

74. Gules, a lion rampant within a bordure indented Or: on a chief argent, three hearts of the first. *Jenkins*

75. Argent, a lion rampant with tail knowed gules, gorged with an Eastern crown Or: in chief, three falcons belled of the third. *Bewes*

76. Argent, two crosses-crosslet fitchy in chief and a horseshoe in base azure: on a chief invected gules, a lion passant of the field. *Adam*

77. Per pale nebuly vert and Or, three pheons in fess between, in chief, a lion passant and another in base counter-passant all counterchanged. *Honan*

78. Gules, three catamounts passant gardant in pale between two flaunches argent each charged with a rose of the first, barbed and seeded proper. *Catt*

79. Gules, a fess ermine, in chief a Bengal tiger passant gardant. *Wallis*

80. Argent, issuant of a fess gules, a demi-lion sable, and in base a fleur-de-lis of the second. *Chalmers*

81. Gules, a lion's head erazed within an orle argent between three crosses potent Or. *Armitage*

82. Argent, on a mount vert a stag lodged proper, on a chief azure three acorns slipped Or. *Broadmead*

83. Sable, a stag trippant between three lance-heads argent. *Jones* (of *Liverpool*)

84. Argent, on a mount vert a stag trippant between two stags erect respecting each other, browsing, and resting their forelegs against as many olive trees all proper. *Weil*

85. Azure, a stag's head caboshed within a bordure dovetailed Or: on a chief wavy ermine, a golden fleece between two spur-rowels of the second. *Dingwall*

86. Per chevron azure and argent, two stags' heads caboshed in chief, and an owl in base counterchanged. *Davies*

87. Per chevron sable and argent, three leopards' faces jessant-de-lis counterchanged. *Huband*

88. Sable, a pall reversed Or between three foxes' heads erazed proper. *Todd.*

89. Ermine, a fess vert fleury-counter-flory Or between three bears' heads couped, sable, muzzled Or. *Simcox*

90. Per pale, vert and gules, a cross botonée Or, on a chief argent, a boar's head couped sable armed and langued gules. *Crombie*

91. Argent, an eagle displayed sable, charged on the breast with a cross paty-fitchy Or between two flaunches of the second each charged with as many billets of the third. *Parkin*

92. Vert, on a cross raguly ermine between, in the first and fourth a garb Or, and in the second and third a

pelican vulning herself, a cross flory of the third between four bezants. *Paget*

93. Argent, a pelican in her piety with wings displayed: a chief dovetailed gules. *Vongall*

94. Sable, a chevron embattled counter-embattled argent guttée d'sang between, in chief two swans respecting each other and, in base, a swan rising, argent: in centre chief a battle-axe Or. *Eastwood*

95. Gules, on a chevron engrailed Or between three swans argent, as many bees volant proper. *Swabey*

96. Argent, on a bend sable, four crosses clechy voided and pommetty of the first: on a chief nebuly azure, a falcon with wings expanded of the field. *Cawston*

97. Per pale azure and sable, two hobbies close in chief proper and in base the sun in his splendour Or. *Hobson*

98. Argent, a chevron gules between three Cornish choughs. *Kirwan*

99. Argent, a cross flory vert between four martlets gules, a chief dovetailed azure. *Bird*

100. Argent, a fess chequy vert and sable between, in chief, two sheldrakes proper and, in base, a lymphad sable. *Linkletter*

101. Upon a wreath of the colours, the moon in her complement issuant from a bank of cloud proper seme of estoiles as in the arms. *Moon*

102. Issuant of a ducal coronet Or, a phoenix in flames of fire proper. *Gray* (of *Newcastle upon Tyne*)

103. Issuant from a circlet of gold embellished with nine pearls raised upon points, a dexter arm in armour embowed grasping in the hand a seax argent. *Lord de Villiers*

104. Upon the battlements of a tower a grouse's leg erazed proper. *Viscount Caldecote* (family name, *Inskip*)

105. Upon a wreath of the colours a cross-crosslet azure surmounted of a thistle, slipped proper. *Dobie of Stonehill*

106. Upon a wreath of the colours a death's head transfixed with a spear in bend sinister, point downward, all proper. *Mackarness*

107. A lion rampant gardant sable supporting a lance erect Or pointed argent within a strap gules fimbriated of the second, buckle and chape gold. *Armorial badge of the blood and name of Clan Gayre*

108. On a chapeau gules turned up ermine, a garb Or supported by two lions rampant the dexter argent the sinister azure. *Lord Amherst of Hackney* (family name, *Cecil*)

109. Upon a wreath of the colours a falcon with wings addorsed Or, armed and membered gules, belled and jessed gold, collared flory-counter-fleury also gules: pendant therefrom a line of roses alternately argent and of the last, all barbed and seeded Or. *Puttock*
   [*Note:* this crest, granted to Col. Geoffrey A. Puttock, 1962 (Wagner, Garter: Portcullis, Pursuivant), is the first in which the bell-thongs and the jesses are shown to be separate.]

110. Out of a ducal coronet Or, a griffin's head azure, beaked and eared gold. *Cornwallis-West*

111. Issuant of an antique crown Or an ostrich's head sable, holding in the beak a horseshoe, gold, between two wings tips elevated, quarterly argent and of the second. *Lord Dudley* (family name, *Smith*)

112. Issuant of a mural crown Or, a wyvern's head sable. *Gawthern*

113. Upon a wreath of the colours a talbot passant argent, collared sable, a line attached thereto passing between the forelegs and reflexed over the back. *Forester*

114. Per pale, and per fess embattled vert and Or; a pen in bend sinister sable between, in the first and fourth quarters, a duck close of the second, each holding in the beak a billet argent. *Billiat*

115. Sable, on a pile erminois, a raven of the field: on a chief nebuly ermine, a griffin sejant Or. *Corbett*

116. Per fess dancetty argent and sable: in chief, a cross of eight points gules between two roses of the last, barbed and seeded proper and, in base, two wings conjoined in leure. *Jacoby*

117. Gules, on a pale between two feathers erect argent, as many of the same, in pale, of the field. *Griggs*

118. Per pale azure and gules three gadflies Or. *Dorre*

119. Per fess azure and gules, a goat's head erazed within an orle or eight martlets argent. *Boord.*

120. Per pale gules and azure a chevron between three herons argent. *Hearn*

121. Gules, a chevron between in chief, two garbs Or and, in base, in bend sinister a flagstaff proper; flotant therefrom in bend, a banner azure, fimbriated of the second and charged with a saltire argent, this being the banner of Scotland. *Alford*

122. Gules on a fess wavy argent between, in chief, a Rhodesian fish-eagle displayed, regardant, Or, grasping in the talons a fish of the second and, in base, a nightape's face gold, a bar wavy azure. *Municipal Corporation of Chingola*

123. Gules, a chevron vairy Or and azure, cotised argent, between three roses of the last barbed and seeded proper. *Reeves*

124. Gules, on a cross invected Or, an oak-tree eradicated proper, between four leopards' faces azure; in the first and fourth quarters a sword erect, and in the second and third a fasces also erect, argent. *Kemball.*

125. Per fess azure and gules, a fess nebuly ermine between two lambs passant in chief argent and, in base, upon a mount proper a dove rising of the fourth, holding in the beak a pea-stalk, the blossom and pods also proper. *Pease*

126. Azure, on each limb of a cross quarterly pierced Or, a chevron gules; and in augmentation of honour, a chief argent; thereon a rose of the third irradiated gold within a wreath of oak-leaves proper. *Whitgreave*

[Thomas Whitgreave of Moseley, Staffordshire, served the Royalist cause, and by his devotion and loyalty did much to preserve and sustain King Charles II after the Battle of Worcester. (The house of Whitgreave, still flourishing, bears also a crest of augmentation.)]

127. Azure, a fess Or fretty gules, two cotises indented of the second between as many cinquefoils in chief and a cross paty-fitchy in base argent. *Bartelot*

128. Per pale gules and azure, three demi-lions passant gardant in pale dimidiated with, and conjoined to, as many demi-hulks of ships, all Or. *Corporation of the Cinque Ports*

129. Azure, on a fess Or a horse courant gules between three mounds, banded of the third. *Moss*

130. Azure, three fleurs-de-lis within a bordure embattled Or, and in augmentation of honour, on a chief of the second, an Eastern crown gules, superscribed 'Khyber', and a canton ermine charged with three cannons fesswise in pale sable. *Pollock*

(The augmentation of honour, including a crest, was granted in respect of distinguished service during the Afghan War.)

131. Per pale azure and fusilly argent and sable: on the dexter a dimidiated eagle displayed, grasping by the string a bugle-horn, all Or, charged on the breast with an antique crown, and, in chief, two crescents of the third. *Lombard*

132. Azure, ten mullets of six points; four, three, two and one Or, within a bordure of the last charged with three fleurs-de-lis gules. *Alston* (of Stockbriggs)

133. Barry wavy of ten argent and azure, a cockatrice displayed Or. *Shaw*

134. Quarterly gules and vert, a fess argent; overall a sword in pale point upward proper pommelled and hilted Or, supported on either side by a kite, gold. *Puttock* . .

135. Barry of twelve azure and argent counterchanged per pale: on a chevron Or, cotised gules three palets of the last each charged with a fleur-de-lis of the third. *Bates*

136. Per fess Or and azure, a pale; three eagles displayed one in chief and two in base, each charged with a cross-crosslet, all counterchanged. *Peacock*

137. Per fess nebuly; in chief checky azure and Or, each of the latter charged with a goutte d'larmes: in base, sable five estoiles, four and one of the second, all within a bordure argent charged with eight crosses humetty, gules. *Corporation of the Borough of Wandsworth*

138. Per fess gules and azure, a fess embattled between, in chief, two hand-grenades Or flammant proper and, in base, an oak-tree fructed of the last. *Inglesby*

139. Pean, on a pile Or, an olive branch fructed. *Gogarty*

140. Argent, a saltire engrailed sable charged with another invected of the field, debruised by an orle azure guttée d'eau: on a chief of the third, three leopards heads erazed proper. *Sills*

141. Per saltire Or and gules, a saltire per saltire counterchanged between, in pale, two ears of wheat slipped and leaved of the first, and, in fess, as many roses of the second, barbed and seeded proper. *Hillborne*

142. Lozengy erminois and sable, on a bend wavy gules three billets argent. *Blundell*

143. Argent a maunch gules bezanty between three keys erect azure debruised by a chevron of the last. *Flavel*

144. Potent argent and azure, on a bend sable two stags' heads caboshed Or. *Thomson*

145. Or, seme of hearts gules; in chief a lion rampant azure. *Gothes*

146. Per fess Or and gules, a fess dovetailed per fess embattled between two falcons belled in chief, and a lion rampant in base, all counterchanged. *Lees* (of Lancashire)

147. Or, seme of estoiles azure a lion rampant gules. *Gallyhalt*

148. Per pale gules and Or a boar passant counterchanged. *Baird of Elie*

149. Or, three bars azure, a double-headed eagle displayed gules. *Walrond*

150. Per pale Or and gules three roundels counterchanged. *D'Abetot*

151. Azure, a dolphin embowed naiant Or, on a chief of the second two saltires couped gules. *Frankland*

152. Barry wavy azure and argent, on a chief of the last, on a cross of St. George a lion of England. *The London County Council*

153. Or, a lion rampant couped at all joints [disjointed] gules within a bordure wavy and quarterly azure and of the second charged, in chief, with a mullet and, in base, a crescent of the first. *Haitland*

154. Argent, a bull passant gules: on a chief azure a sword and a key respectively point and wards upward, in saltire, between two harps of the field. *Bovey*

155. Per chevron argent and azure, in chief two towers sable and, in base, a horse forcene of the first. *Madge*

156. Ermine, on a fess nebuly gules, three quatrefoils argent, and, in chief, a greyhound courant sable. *Hayne*

157. Per fess azure and sable, three crescents in fess between as many hedgehogs passant argent. *Harris*

158. Per pale argent and sable, three chevronells engrailed between as many brocks all counterchanged. *Brocklehurst*

159. Sable, a wolf rampant Or, between, in chief, two mitres argent. *Lowth*

160. Per pale gules and vert, an elephant statant and on his back a castle triple-towered and domed Or. *Corporation of the City of Coventry*

161. Or, a fess chequy azure and argent, surmounted of a bend engrailed gules, charged with three salmon hauriant of the first, in sinister chief point a buckle, all within a double tressure flory-counter-fleury of the fourth. *Stewart:* (being I & IV in *McTaggart-Stewart*)

162. Argent, three salmon hauriant gules; in chief, an oak-tree eradicated proper. *Cain*

163. Azure, three trout interlaced in triangle, one naiant, one urinant in bend, and one hauriant in bend sinister, all argent. *Troutbeck*

164. Barry-wavy argent and gules, six crevices Or, three, two and one. *Atwater*

165. Argent, three crabs erect gules. *Alvanston*

166. Sable, a cross floretty engrailed between four escallops argent. *Fletcher*

167. Per fess indented argent and gules, a pale with three whelk-shells two and one, and as many storks one and two, all counterchanged. *Storey*

168. Argent, a sword in bend entwined with a serpent all proper between two bendlets vert. *Dooner*

169. Ermine, three harvest-flies gules. *Chettle*

170. Argent, three butterflies in pale sable. *Bolour .*

171. Gules, a pale argent surmounted of a chevron invected counterchanged between two escutcheons in chief, of the second and, in base, one of the first, each charged with a bee, volant, proper. *Sewell*

172. Sable, a unicorn statant Or: on a chief of the last three billets of the first. *Styleman*; (being both 2 and 3 sub-quarters and II grand quarter of *Le Strange*)

173. Sable, on a pile Or, between two roses argent barbed and seeded proper a wyvern vert. *Hinchcliffe*

174. Argent, a bull passant sable armed and unguled Or, within a bordure of the second, charged with eight bezants; on a canton sinister per pale gules and azure, a harp of the third stringed argent: ensigned with an Earl's coronet, issuant therefrom a helmet befitting his degree and, mantled of his liveries whereon is set, upon a wreath of the colours, his crest, viz., upon a wreath of the colours a demi-dragon, wings elevated, vert; holding a dart in the dexter claw and resting the sinister on an antique buckler, charged as the canton.

Supporters: Two dragons regardant vert, each holding in the inner foreclaw a dart. *Earl of Enniskillen, Baron Grinstead* (family name, *Cole*)

175. Azure, issuant from the centre of a bar wavy of water proper in the nombril-point, a bridge of three arches embattled, argent, masoned sable, the whole between as many sea-lions, each crowned with a naval crown, Or. *Bridge*

176. Per saltire argent and azure, in chief, a sea lion sejant and, in base, a fleur-de-lis both sable: in the flanks two garbs Or, and in the fess point a crescent of the third for difference. *Lowson*

177. Argent, a saltire invected between four roses gules. *Macfarlane-Grieve.* (First and fourth quarter)

178. Or, on a saltire gules a thistle slipped proper, on a chief of the second a maple-leaf between two shamrocks, also proper. *Bruce*

179. Argent, a chevron azure between, in chief, two sprigs of lime and, in base, one of jute, all fructed proper. *Brown* (London)

180. Chevrony of six Or and gules a holly-tree proper fructed of the second. *Clare*

181. Argent, on a mount vert a cotton-tree fructed proper: on a chief azure, between two bezants, an escutcheon of the field charged with a bee volant proper. *Arkwright*

182. Lozengy ermine and sable, on a chief of the last, three garden-lilies argent, slipped and seeded Or. *Magdalen College, Oxford*

183. Vert, on a pale between two cinquefoils argent, a fir-tree eradicated proper. *Melles*

184. Azure, a cinquefoil between three ears of wheat slipped and leaved, two in chief and one in base, and as many estoiles one in chief and two in base, all Or. *Trist*

185. Argent, a chevron ermines between two branches of oak fructed and slipped in chief, and an esquire's helmet in base, all proper. *Robinson*

186. Or, a chevron chequy argent and sable, between three water-bougets of the third: in centre chief a rose gules. *Ross*

187. Or, on a chevron gules three escutcheons argent, each charged with a bluebottle slipped and leaved proper: on a chief of the second a crown vallery of the first. *Municipal Corporation of Chorley, Lancashire*

188. Argent a chevron sable between three gillyflowers proper. *Skevington*

189. Or, on a chevron azure, between three sheaves of holly banded gules, an anchor cabled of the first between two dolphins embowed proper. *Irvine*

190. Ermine, a chevron engrailed sable, between three chaplets of roses proper: a chief vert fretty argent. *Burra*

191. Or, on a fess gules, between three branches of birch slipped proper, a mirror pometty argent. *Birkmyre* . .

192. Per pale ermine and azure, two bars indented each charged with three pears slipped, all counterchanged. *Perryman*

193. Per chevron Or and azure a wreath of oak vert be-

tween, in chief, two estoiles of the second and, in base, a cross patonce of the first. *Leeming*

194. Azure a basket of fruit proper between three mitres Or. *Jann*

195. Per fess gules and sable, a tower triple-towered Or between two flaunches argent each charged with a cinquefoil of the first. *Jones of Bealanamore*

196. Or, three caltraps and a chief sable. *Devie*

197. Azure, three field-pieces on their carriages in pale Or, on a chief argent as many cannonballs sable. *Army Ordnance Office*

198. Or, guttée d'poix, on a fess nebuly gules, between four bombs fired, three in chief and one in base proper, an escallop between two Catherine-wheels Or. *Cartwright* (Ireland)

199. Ermine, a fess Or between, in chief, two wolves' heads erazed sable and, in base, as many swords in saltire proper, the pommels and hilts of the second. *Cartwright* (Canada)

200. Per pale argent and gules, in pale a sword erect proper, pommelled and hilted Or between two lions combatant counterchanged. *Carrol*

201. Or, five swords in pale counterpoised fesswise proper, pommelled and hilted sable: on a chief invected of the last, three escallops of the field. *Graham*

202. Sable, four swords interlaced fret-wise argent hilted and pommelled Or: on a chief of the second two crosses humetty gules. *Goss*

203. Per fess argent and azure, in chief, a falcon's head issuant of a heart proper between two mullets of the second: in base, as many claymores in saltire points baseward proper, entwined at the point of intersection with a serpent involved, facing the sinister, Or. *Falconer*

204. Argent, two tilting spears in saltire proper between four ermine spots sable within a bordure chequy gules and of the field. *Craufurd*

205. Per saltire azure and sable,* a cross paty between four pheons, two in pale and two in fess Or. *Ward*

206. Per pale argent and gules, two bird-bolts in saltire, surmounted in the centre by a tun, between three roses all counterchanged. *Bolton*

207. Argent, three sheaves of as many arrows proper banded gules, on a chief azure, a bee volant, Or. *Peel*

208. Gules, two keys addorsed in bend, the upper Or, the lower argent, interlaced with a sword in bend sinister, surmounting the lower, and surmounted by the upper, of the third pommelled and hilted of the second. (*See of Winchester*)

209. Sable, two chevronells between, in chief, two water-bougets and, in base, a demi-sun issuant, all Or. *Meeks*

210. Per saltire, in chief and in base gules, dexter and sinister sable* all guttée d'eau: a lion passant between four scaling ladders Or. *Morris*

211. Per fess Or and argent, a lymphad sable, the sail furled; pendant from the sinister end thereof an escutcheon gules charged with a trefoil of the second. *M'Echarn*

212. Argent, on a bend wavy azure between two lymphads sable, flags flying and oars over the side, an anchor cabled Or. *Conder*

213. Quarterly, per fess wavy: I, argent a cross gules; II and III ermine, and IV chequy Or and azure; overall, a pale sable, thereon a crosier ensigned with a mitre of

* Nos. 205 and 210: observe the two different modes of expression.

the third all within a bordure of the fifth charged with fifteen bezants. *Corporation of the Borough of Lambeth*

214. Ermine, a pall azure charged with the crosier of St. Fillan, Or. *Dewar*

215. Argent, on a chevron between, in chief, two church-bells and, in base, a nag's head erazed azure, bridled Or, three pairs of hands couped at the wrist, in saltire, palm to palm proper. *Clapton* (of Stamford)

216. Argent, a millrind gules within an orle of eight mill-rinds sable. *Milne*

217. Gules, three keys erect Or each enfiled with a ducal coronet of the same. *Orford*

218. Ermine, on a pale engrailed azure between two keys, the dexter inverted, the sinister inverted and reversed Or, a quill pen, pale-wise, argent. *Chartered Institute of Secretaries*

219. Gules, on a chevron argent between three pairs of barley-garbs in saltire of the second, banded of the same, as many tuns sable, hooped Or. *Worshipful Company of Brewers*

220. Azure a chevron between three hanks of cotton argent. *Cotton*

220A. Azure, on a fess between three battle-axes erect, argent, as many escallops gules: ensigned with an eccle-siastical hat corded and tasselled of one tassel on each side, sable. *Wright*

220B. Or, a maunch gules. *Lord Hastings.* (Fourth quarter – family name, *Astley*)

221. Sable, on a chevron engrailed between three chess-rooks argent, as many crosses-crosslet fitchy of the first. *Warter*

222. Gules, three dice proper each charged with six spots in front, three on the sinister and two on top. *Mathias*

223. Azure, a portcullis Or, on a chief of the last, on a pale between two Tudor Roses, the Arms attributed to King Edward the Confessor, namely: azure a cross patonce between five martlets, two, two and one, all Or. *Corporation of the City of Westminster*

224. Per fess, in chief the Royal Arms of Great Britain and Northern Ireland: in base, Or, an open book proper inscribed with the word 'Scientia'. *Imperial College of Science and Technology* (London). Grant by Royal Warrant of King Edward VII

225. Or, two bars and, in chief as many crosses paty fitchy sable, ensigned with a helmet befitting his degree and, for his crest, upon a wreath of the colours a talbot's head erazed sable, mantled sable doubled Or: pendant from its ribbon beneath the shield the Cross of [an Order of Chivalry]

226. Argent, on a chevron between three dolphins naiant embowed sable, a marguerite proper between two naval crowns Or: an escutcheon of pretence per pale Or and gules, on a bend between two talbots' heads erazed, three ash-leaves, all counterchanged. *Sargent*, with, in pretence, *Ashman*

227. Quarterly, I and IV argent two bars raguly between four crosses-crosslet fitchy in chief and a falcon belled in base all gules (for Lees), II, argent, on a bend in-vected plain double cottised sable guttée d'eau, three eagles each with two heads displayed ermine (for Brown), III, gules, on a bend invected erminois between two bezants three martlets azure all within a bordure ermine (for Collins) *Lees of Thurland Castle*

228. Azure, in base barry wavy of four argent and of the first; issuant therefrom an iceberg proper: on a chief of the second three eggs, also proper: ensigned with a Baron's coronet, issuant therefrom a helmet befitting his degree and, for his Crest, upon a wreath of the colours, in front of a springbok's head couped at the neck proper three mullets fess-wise azure: Supporters, dexter, a sheep proper; sinister a bull argent. *Lord Vestey*

229. Gules, on a chief argent two mullets sable, pierced round, of the field. On an escutcheon in centre chief, the Badge of Ulster. *Bacon, Sir E. C.* (Premier Baronet of England)

230. Chequy argent and sable, a fess gules. On a dexter caton the Badge of Ulster. *Acland, Sir R. T. D.* (fifteenth Baronet)

Note: Blazons No. 7 and 225. The former is of a spurious achievement, and the latter, having been altered from what was submitted, is merely fictitious. The author regrets the inclusion of these, but the deceptions were not discovered in time to eliminate them: however, that good may come of it, we have incorporated No. 225 in a book-plate, for these little works of art provide a subject in which a student of Heraldry may specialize.

Appendix

ALL heraldic drawing demands a high skill if the work is to be
for public exhibition: it is regrettable that so much of it is
shocking. The human form in heraldry generally appears most
stodgy and wooden since human beings cannot assume poses as
rampant or passant: only the true heraldic artist – very few and
far between – can impart to the human form the dignity and
grace coupled to the symbolic attitude needed to give such
supporters (or charges) the Gothic appeal to eye, mind and
emotions that such figures ought to have, even when of classic
origin.

The reader is most particularly asked to note that the foregoing comment refers to drawings that will be exhibited – profes-
sional work – not to private notebooks. It is, as a matter of fact,
desirable that every student of heraldry, no matter how super-
ficial may be his (or her) interest, begins to make drawings of
shields, and either fills them in with coloured pencil, or, if able,
paints them. Many a person who cannot draw – including the
author – has found that there is great fun to be had in 'doing'
coats of arms.

On a visit to a country house, a church or a cathedral, one
can make rough sketches of the arms seen and 'trick' the colours.
Tricking is the classic method of making heraldic notes. One
simply uses accepted abbreviations and writes these in or, if the
space is too small, writes them outside the shield and carries an
arrow in. The standard abbreviations for tricking are as follows:

A or arg = argent: O or Or = Or: V or ver = vert:
B = azure (this is to avoid confusion with argent): G or gu =
gules: S or sa = sable: P or purp = purpure. The furs are
best written in full if used, but their elements can be tricked;
this is simple enough. Draw the shield and scribble in indications
of ermine spots. On the field can appear A, or O, or S; an arrow
to one of the points can indicate sa, Or, arg. The same plan
applies to vair: trick the metal and tincture in the first two bells.

The Officers of Arms themselves, in making rough sketches
in notebooks, have always used tricking, not cross-hatching.
Heraldic display is a glory of contrasting colour, and should be
so visualized; however, the cross-hatching system blinded the
draughtsmen of the past so that they could not conceive of a coat
of arms depicted without it.

It is useful to know the code, but the student must think in
colour, not in dots and dashes. In giving the meaning of these
scratches we are deliberately using non-heraldic terms for the

colours: silver is left blank: gold is represented by dots all over the place: red, by lines in pale; blue, by lines in fess: black by a mixture of these giving a network of squares: green has lines in bend: purple in bend sinister.

Now and then, in drawing, these lines are useful: for example, on roundels, but the modern tendency is to abandon them in favour of strong expressive drawing: those who wish to know the colours and who are learned in heraldry, will look up the blazon: those who are not interested are most certainly unlikely to be inspired to inquire because the general effect has been spoiled by criss-cross lines.

Index

Read this before using the Index

The following index will help the reader in three ways: first, to find material in the text; secondly, to find graphic representation of the figures in the illustrations; and thirdly, by indicating the usage of the language of Heraldry expressed in blazon.

After most items there are two groups of figures. Those in light type refer to the numbers of the illustrations, those in bold type refer to the page number where the item is introduced in the text: thus: nebuly: 30, 38, 65, 77, 96, 115, 125, 137, 156, **27**; hence, if after reading the description of nebuly on page **27** one wishes to see it at work, it will be found at each illustration represented by the light figures.

After having looked at it doing almost everything it can do, one may wish to confirm its expression in words. To do this, look up 'Blazon of Illustration', where the numbers conform to the drawings.